One Who Flew Into the Cuckoo's Nest

GINGER PENDO

Copyright © 2025 Ginger Pendo
All rights reserved
First Edition

PAGE PUBLISHING
Meadville, PA

First originally published by Page Publishing 2025

ISBN 979-8-89922-197-2 (pbk)
ISBN 979-8-89922-221-4 (digital)

Printed in the United States of America

Acknowledgments

Professor Paul Aamot told us we would be learning his own English teaching. It was completely different! I was terrified of writing. I never learned English in high school. Professor Paul taught me and gave me the courage to try to write my story. Years later, Professor Paul died in 2010. I found his son, also a professor, Gregg Aamot, among the English faculty at Ridgewater (Willmar Community College back in '81).

His son, Gregg, emailed me a brief note explaining his father's idea of teaching:

> I am sure you had a lot of good teachers then, but when the note mentioned that your teacher had a unique method to teaching English I wondered if you were referring to my father, Paul Aamot. He used a few textbooks that he wrote himself (*Composition 500, Writing Insights*) as well as his own handouts. His methods were different than those of most teachers. One of his methods was to teach sentence structure by boiling them down to four parts that students could easily remember:

the "main part" of the sentence (the independent clause) along with three subordinate clauses that he called "introductions," "interruptions," and "extensions." Maybe that sounds familiar?

He was my English teacher. Professor Paul was much simpler. He made us write a lot. I got A's on all my papers. On the last day of my English class, I got up enough nerve to ask Professor Paul Aamot, "How could I get all A's! My English isn't that good?"

He looked me square in my eyes and just replied, "I liked your writing. You have a gift. You are a very powerful writer. You write straight from your heart. Let the editors clean up your punctuation and very small amount of your grammar. Don't let their grammar override your grammar. Know this. You could write a masterpiece. Keep writing."

Well, about fifty years later, I started writing my memoirs. I could hear him pushing me! I feel so sorry and sad for a son's loss of his father, a great man! My classmates and I thought your father was great. He gave most of us the courage to write without years of studying English!

Sister Mary Rachel Kubelbeck was my professor in nursing. She found me and called me over twenty years after I graduated. I was shocked and asked her how she could remember me and how she found me. Her response was, "I never forgot you as a student. I wanted to know how your life went." To this day, we are very close. I went up and stayed with her for a few days. I told her about my nursing experiences. I talked with her about writing my memoirs. She pushed me hard to write and, I mean, really pushed in her soft way. I talked about my doubts, about my lack of English. She brushed that very quickly aside and told me to write. By the time I left, she made me feel like I had to write, or I would disappoint her. I just couldn't let her down. She stayed pushing me all these past three years. She read all my work as I wrote. She was so encouraging. I never would have made it without her believing in me. What a professor! I love you, Sister Mary!

Jeanmarie Murry was my gift from God. She came into my life three years ago. She was and is my next-door neighbor. I didn't know her. I was outside in the yard, asking another neighbor if she knew of anybody that knew English. Jeanmarie was outside, and she overheard me talking. She came over, walked right up to me, and said "You'll need me. I am an English teacher. I've been teaching English for forty years, and I will help you write your story." We've been together almost every week for three years. We are very close. I thank God every day for her help. I couldn't have done it without her! She is a marvelous teacher. Jeanmarie never wrote or told me what to write. She would simply say something like, "Doesn't that paragraph sound off to you. What do you think?" I would say, "Yuck, that doesn't sound right. I'll rewrite it!" Then when I finished, Jeanmarie would respond, "You got it!" She also shared that I opened the prior unbeknownst to her—the world of acute psychiatric illness and the appropriate use of patient restraints. The use of such restraints made both patients and staff safe.

Judy Entz entered our lives at the end of writing our memoirs. Judy just picked us up and carried us to the final ending of creating chapter and titles. That took a lot of exhausting effort and time from her. We were just too exhausted. She kept telling us we could get our work finished together. We wouldn't have been able to finish the memoirs. Neither I nor Jeanmarie knew how to do chapters! We owed Judy a lot. We want her to know how much of what she did for us was appreciated. We promised to get to meet each other this summer for lunch!

William S. Whorton, my brother Bill, lives in Thailand. He has a master's in educational foundations and philosophy. He has spent twenty-four years translating *The Bhagavad Gita*, which a publisher wanted. My brother gave it to him for free. It was doing quite well. I asked him to help me with my memoir. At first, he was a little incredulous. "Kid, you don't have any English. You can't write." I told my brother, "I just have to try."

He immediately said, "I will support you anyway I can!" I sent my memoir to him. His response was, "As promised, I carefully read your great work. Overall, I believe it is great. You are a very powerful writer and storyteller. You have a real writing gift of brilliant use of examples and illustrations and metaphors to give your writing power and clarity. This is very impressive." He helped me so much!

Here I'll speak for myself. I can't say that I never made a mistake. The beauty in our hospital unit of when making a mistake, I was laughed at or teased unmercifully! Never once did anybody get angry with me or try to make me feel stupid or not part of the team. We talked about corrections to help a person learn. Such kindness was normal, and that same kindness was shown to our patients who were at times hell-bent on destroying us through no fault of their own insanity.

My brother was a marine in Vietnam. So many stories. Out of all his stories, he talked about the battlefield. Marines had a battlefield mentality of "all for one and one for all!" They never left a dead man on the battlefield, no matter how dangerous or how more lives were lost. No marine was left on the battlefield!

Here I create an analogy: Our work was extremely dangerous many times. The staff as soldiers, some with gut-wrenching, instantaneous fleeting fear pushed aside everything to do their job. We had to be together. Our takedowns many times were hard. We always had to work as one for! We tried to protect our patients. We deeply cared for them. They were innocent people, just horribly sick. Our job was to get them to where they had control over their sanity. We felt our patients' mental anguish. They came in without any control over their sanity. None!

I had the chance to work with the finest caring people. I feel sad for all the people who will never have the chance to work with such great people. I am asking for understanding of a staff that works tirelessly every workday to help these patients stuck in their horrible mental psychotic pain.

I have wonderful memoirs of working with you all. I miss you!

Born in 1945, I am now an old lady of eighty years, looking back over my life of a wide variety of pathways—openings and closings. In my years ranging from birth to the age of five, my promising normal life suddenly, very cruelly, and abruptly made a sharp turn. All my pathways were completely closed, leaving me with only one pathway! Finally, at the age of thirty-two, a bewildering revelation gave back to me all of life's pathways, which once more opened life up for me. Out of that miracle, I was able to fulfill my dream of being a nurse, getting my BSN(Bachelor of Science degree in nursing) and becoming a Registered Nurse. From graduation to the "Wings of Faith," I ended up as an acute psychiatric nurse at the Queen's Medical Hospital in downtown Honolulu, Hawaii. This hospital was founded in 1859 by Queen Emma for all her Hawaiian people. In this hospital, the behavioral unit, Kekela, was divided into two units with two separate nursing stations: Makai, with regular locked glass doors, and Mauka, with big windowless locked steel doors.

Looking back, remembering the first time I walked through Makai, and through the steel doors of Mauka, my heart started pumping wildly. I could even hear my heart pumping in my ears.

As the steel doors shut, I started walking down a very long and wide hallway. Suddenly, there were human beings in a big room. They were very different beings than I had seen before. They were a jumbled mass of humanity insanity! My first instinct was raw and overwhelming fear and then just, "Get me out of here!" I wanted to turn and run away and go home. To myself, I said, *Think, Ginger. You can't run. You have a job, and you can't get any other nursing jobs.* What am I supposed to do? Facing reality in a world of no reality, I continued, *I don't even know what to say to these people. I don't even know if I could touch them! Well, I guess you'll just have to learn!*

I am asking the readers of this story to try having an open mind and an open heart to feel for these human beings. If my reader is already acquainted with or caring for people having an acute psychotic mental illness, to them I would say you have my deepest sense of empathy and admiration. My patients were always, for me, human beings, who, through no fault of their own, were born with psychotic abnormalities. Some of my patients, by their own hands, used drugs or alcohol that permanently destroyed their brains. It didn't make any difference that they were all human beings; they were treated by most of society as human garbage! This, I believe, is simply because people aren't aware of their reality. The normal society simply becomes afraid of these strange people when they're not in a full psychotic breakdown. People simply turn their heads while pretending they aren't there, hence, they don't exist.

I am writing this story to debunk what the normal population may think about mental illness as described in the book and movie, *One Who Flew Over the Cuckoo's Nest*. In contrast, I am describing the reality to the *One Who flew Into the Cuckoo's Nest*! My patients were, in a more common language, carrying the standard patient's nomenclature of total insanity. Many times they are referred to as, "That person is totally crazy!" This story is to open up why the USA is so far behind in caring for these people. Our movies, I also remember all too well, show mental health units, emphasizing how the patients looked more mentally healthy than the staff. The staff were portrayed as the enemy of the patients. One of the first stories about mental health that I can remember was titled, *The Snake Pit*. Later, one of the country's favorite books was made into a movie, *One Flew Over the Cuckoo's Nest*, in which worked the tyrannical Nurse Ratchet. She was a very mean person. Hence, all nurses and staff working today are mean, unfeeling, and horrible people, in contrast to the patients who are nice, polite, and sane people who are just misunderstood! This is a lie!

In all the years I worked with the most dangerous patients, not once did I ever see or experience disrespect or lack of caring from the staff when working with our patients. We felt great empathy toward our patients! It was so sad to see human beings so sick, and we responded to them knowing we had to help them get better! We understood mental illness is extremely painful, no different than a physical pain, and there was nothing we could do to eliminate their lifetime of pain! There was no medicine, unlike today we have medication which can help them. We can only get patients to baseline behavior and then have to release them back into society, most of the time into a very uncaring society.

I want to start with a short prologue of my life to let my reader know who I am to write this story. At my birth, my life started with so many promising pathways, more than I could ever think about. All of life's pathways were there for the taking. Then suddenly, in my fifth year, they were all gone.

Born in 1908, my mother, Helen Whorton, at the age of nineteen in 1927, went to work at Fort Riley, Kansas, in civil service. Fort Riley had just initiated a test run to determine if a female could succeed in fulfilling a secretary's occupation. She was a beacon of hope for future women. This was a time when no female could be a secretary due to a perceived inborn lack of intellectual abilities for all females. Only men were deemed intelligent. She was a woman completely ahead of her time. Mama was a woman who spent her life on her own terms: independent and self-reliant. We always teased Mama about how she flunked motherhood and housekeeping. However, when it came to fatherhood and being a provider, she got all As, plus, plus! She would say, "Yep, that's me." Then we would start laughing. Somewhere in the 1960s, Mama became the Purchasing and Contracting Officer for Fort Riley, Kansas. Mama was given several honors for becoming the number one ranking civilian at Fort Riley and expert for purchasing contracting throughout the 5th Army!

Mama sat me down at age five, just before entering kindergarten, and explained to me the status of my mental capacities. Carefully, she described how her brain worked like my brother's, how she and my brother loved to read and learn. In contrast, my brain loved to work with my hands. She told me it might be hard for me to learn what would be taught at school but to remember always that my gift would be to learn to work with my hands. In other words, something was wrong with my brain.

After Mama's talk, I went up the stairs to my room, grabbing my cat, Muffin. I closed the door, threw Muffin on my bed, crawled up on the bed, and buried my head into her soft fur. Muffin started to lick my hair, and I just cried and cried until I was exhausted and fell asleep. When I woke up, I felt like somebody had ripped out half my heart and brain. I was so torn apart. It was horrible. When I got up later, I went to my brother and cried, and he was, as always, mean to me. He stated to me in clear pear-shaped words, "Yeah, kid. Face it. You're retarded. You're just plain stupid!" All those words from my mother and my brother are, to this day, permanently stamped into my brain.

That's it. I'm out of here. With that, I walked out of the house. My legs felt so weak while crying. I kept falling, tripping over my weak legs, banging up my knees and hands on the then gravel road. All I kept thinking was I have to get to Lady's, my wonderful godmother. When I was born, she was seventy-five years old, born in 1875. Lady always said, "The first time I laid eyes on you, I knew I was done for. I'm way too old for this, but you'll need me. As long as I can, I'll always be here for you."

When I walked through the door, I was crying. Lady took one look at me, took hold of my hand, and sat down on the couch, pulling me onto her lap. While holding me with her wonderful warm arms, placing her head on mine, rocking me, holding me gently, whispering until I fell asleep again, "Shh, shh, you're safe now. It's alright." She never talked much, but she always showed me so much love.

I stayed there a couple of weeks. I never told her what had been said to me. She never asked. She just showered me with love. Lady never questioned me or talked about my home. She, in her own quiet way, just let me know that when I was with her, I would always be safe and loved. But she rarely used the word *love*. Just by lots of hugs, touch, and caring, she showed her love. She was quite a beautiful human being, and I still, to this day, love her and thank her for all that she gave me. When I left, my heart was healed, and my mind accepted my retardation. I still had a life to live. I never told another soul as it was always my secret. Now that I am in my seventies, I feel safe talking about it.

I will add here that Lady was born before Social Security. She was financially destitute. My mother financially took care of her monetary needs. Like Mama said, "I work twelve to fourteen hours a day, five days a week, and on the weekends, four to eight hours on many Saturdays and Sundays." Remember, my mother worked in a male-dominated world. "I knew there was no way I could meet my daughter's needs. I always knew you would be safe with Lady. She loved you so much, and you loved her. That's a gift. I knew that and I could make that happen."

With deep conviction, my mother probably said to Lady regarding her financial situation, "Lady, I'll never ever have to watch you getting hauled off to the poor house!" Mama kept Lady and our grandma financially secure until the day they died. Mama also paid for their funerals and burials.

Much later, when my brother and I were in our fifties, we became very close in taking care of our mother. Our mother got top-notch care for her last four years of life. Mama was told every day she was loved, and every day she got loving care. Today, my brother is like a rock for me. We have great love and respect for each other. For my brother, it's a little more respect than love, and for me, it's a little more love than respect; however, it's solid. We never ever speak to each other in anger. We can always talk through anything together with understanding. This is the safest relationship one can have! It's a wonderful gift.

Like Mama said, I could learn to clean, sew, and be a good wife to a man who would have to provide for me. Well, there were no more thoughts or choices to any of life's multitude of pathways. They were gone. I could only have one pathway, always inferior. From that day on, I didn't bother going to school very much, because after all, I couldn't learn. I did manage to graduate from Chapman, Kansas, in 1963, ninety-fifth from the bottom, out of the class of ninety-six. I was raised in Junction City, Kansas, but was kicked out of high school in my junior year for not showing up to classes, hence the move to Chapman. From then on, there was nothing but to follow that singular path. So I got married at age eighteen and had my first baby at nineteen. I had two more children after that. I worked as a waitress, store clerk, and on a turkey line eviscerating turkey gullet. That was the worst job I ever had. One thing I did notice was there weren't any white people there—all Mexican immigrants.

What Have I Done?

~~~~~~~~~~~~~~~~

For whatever reason, I was bored with raising kids, cooking (which I've always disliked), and cleaning. At the grand old age of thirty-two, I was vacuuming the living room floor, the kids were in school, and I got to thinking about my life. My life was dull, nothing to look forward to, feeling sorry for myself, and my lot in life. Suddenly, I wondered, *Am I retarded?* I had never challenged this. I never tried, but I always wanted to be a nurse. So throwing down my vacuum, I jumped in the car, and drove from Litchfield, Minnesota, to Willmar, Minnesota, which was about twenty miles away. Finding Willmar Community College, today known as Ridgewater College, I went in and signed up for a chemistry course. This occurred about the late 1970s to early 1980s.

Shaking and scared, I was fearfully thinking all the way home, *What have you done? You actually signed up for a chemistry course— have you lost your ever-loving mind?* Yet I had always been told, if you wanted to be a nurse, you had to learn chemistry. By the time I got home, my mind was swirling with the memory of all the years of being "less than," always being retarded, unable to have a drop of hope. I told myself, *You're stupid. What makes you think you can pretend to be smart? Do you need to prove you're stupid again? I don't know.*

I just have to prove once and for all, to my own satisfaction about my mental abilities or lack thereof. Arriving back home, I jumped out of the car and raced into the house to call my Mama.

When she answered, the first words out of my mouth were "Mama, guess what I did today?"

Her response was "I don't know, honey, what you did today?"

Gushing out, my response gushing was "I went to Willmar Community College and signed up for a course in chemistry!"

Her response was "You did what? Oh, honey, honey, you can't take chemistry. You haven't even had algebra. Chemistry is hard, with lots of equations. It's very mathematical. There is no way you can pass. Why would you want to hurt yourself?"

Crying now, I spoke, "Mama, Mama, I just have to try. I need your support, Mama. Please, Mama, tell me you will support me, please."

Mama, with a deeply sad voice, stated, "Okay, sweetheart, I'll support you."

Tears pouring out of my eyes, I responded, "Thank you, Mama. I need money to replace the money I spent on the course. It was my grocery money."

Mama said, "Okay, honey, I'll send you money."

My eldest daughter, Debby, a teenager who was a mathematical genius, taught her mother algebra. I studied hard and finished the chemistry course. Then I called my mother with the news.

"Mama, guess what? I made an A in chemistry!"

The phone call went like this, with Mama's response, "WOW! Oh my word! How is this possible?" Then the phone went dead. I could tell she hadn't hung up. I called her name. No response.

Then I waited again, and I said, "Mama, are you there? Talk to me?"

Finally, her voice came, and she said, "How can you ever, ever, ever forgive me?"

My response was "Mama, I forgive you. I love you."

She went on to say, "Sweetheart, I took a lot of theoretical chemistry. I would never have made it through mathematical chemistry. Sweetheart, do you realize you're smarter than I am or even your brother?"

We talked for a long time. Suddenly, my world opened to all the normal pathways of life! Not only did I earn this A but I was also on dean's list for the next four years. For the fifth year, I only missed dean's list by just a couple of points. At that time, I was just really exhausted, and my two girls were fighting a lot. I was constantly being interrupted. I just couldn't get any alone time for studies.

Well, the biggest part of my life opened. However, there was still the world I had built as a retarded person. This became my day-to-day reality test. I had three children to care for and raise, no help from the father, a house with floors and bathrooms, a kitchen to clean, along with the weekly bedding to be changed and clothes had to be washed and put away. In that time, the late '70s, we carried a lot of the old values such as husbands were never expected to lift a finger to clean or cook. So that also left me with the responsibility of having supper on the table at 5:00 p.m. Along with that, I had a part-time graveyard job. It would take me about seven years to get to graduation—five years part-time at Willmar Community College and two years full time at the College of St. Benedict's nursing program. In 1984, I got my BSN.

Two weeks after my graduation, and two weeks before having to take the Nursing State Boards Test, my husband came through the door for supper, stood at the table, and made an announcement, "I don't love you. I want a divorce, and Litchfield is the town where I was born and raised in, so I'm going to stay here. It might get uncomfortable for you. You might want to go to your mom in Hawaii!"

WHOA! We were married for twenty-one years! Well, that tidbit of news destroyed me! I was way more than upset. I was a walking, talking basket case. First thing I thought of was *What am I going to do about my upcoming nursing boards test?* I could barely talk, let alone think. Later, I found out my best friend wanted my husband for herself and started having an affair with him. That piece of information is still torturous to my soul to this day!

Two weeks went by, lying in bed about five in the morning, I suddenly thought, *Damn! Today is test day!* I have to get to Minneapolis, which was about an hour and a half drive!

No car, I called all over town and found the car and my husband at my best friend's house, and I screamed at him, "Get the car and get me down to Minneapolis now!"

I continued to scream and cried the whole trip to Minneapolis. At the auditorium, I ran and got through the door as it was shutting behind me. I was a mess in old shorts, unwashed shirt, hair not combed, red eyes still crying, and snot running out of my nose! I just froze standing there, not moving. A couple of girls from my classes spotted me and came racing over to me. No time for explanations. They sat me down, gave me wad of Kleenex, a pencil, a quick pat on back, and stated, "You can do this, Ginger!"

I can't remember much of what happened after that. That night, my mother had made arrangements for a hotel across the street from the auditorium to stay for the two days of testing. My classmates were staying there also. All I can remember was they never left me alone, and somewhere along the line, I had clean clothes.

To this day, I say, "Thank you. You girls helped me in an hour of crisis need like none other!"

With the test over, I had to leave town, commonly known as going back home to Mama, who had retired from her job of approximately forty-seven years at Fort Riley. Mama moved from her home in Junction City, Kansas, to set up her new home in Kaneohe, Hawaii. So off I went to Hawaii to be with my Mama. Of course, she also bought the plane ticket. We both knew there was no way I could have passed my state boards. I would have to wait till fall to get my test results. I landed in Hawaii on a Friday night, and by the following Monday, I was working in a nursing home, taking care of an elderly lady. The rest was just waiting time until the state boards were released. I would just sit and stare at the walls. Mama would pull me out every day for supper.

Mama had never learned to cook, but she brought me flowers. She kept telling me, "You will get over this. I promise you."

After months of waiting, my state boards results were sent to me. With jaw dropping excitement, I hollered, "I did it! I passed my boards!"

Review Leaving the World of Sanity

———— ⚘ ————

It was 1984 when the biggest changes for all future medical care took place. Insurance companies, through DRGs (Diagnostics Related Groups), took over physicians', hospitals', and patients' care! The first thing they cut was the number of days patients could stay in the hospital. Before this, physicians had always given orders for patients' length of stay. Now for each diagnosis, there was a fixed number of days anybody could stay in a hospital, no matter what the physicians or patients wanted. The result of this was that hospitals' census fell through the floor, resulting in thousands of nurses getting laid off, along with many hospitals closing throughout the country. Today, physicians are not allowed to use their professional judgment. Insurance companies make most of our medical care decisions through Policy and Procedures! As a new graduate, I was scared of ever getting a nursing job. I was stymied, or in normal words, SOL!

Then in the Honolulu newspaper, there was an ad for nurses and new graduates. This was unbelievable when there were thousands of seasoned nurses laid off. "Oh well, Queen's Hospital in Honolulu, had an ad for new graduates."

Next day, I borrowed Mama's car, drove to the massive Queen's Hospital, had my interview with the nurse managers for the psychiatric unit, and was told that I had the job, if all my paperwork cleared. Though I was thrilled with the thought of a nursing job, I was slightly down because psychiatric units during nursing school were boring. Scolding myself for my thoughts, I reminded myself that when things got better, I could look for a better nursing job!

In 1984, Queen's Hospital was the only hospital in all of Hawaii with locked psychiatric units. So the worst of the dangerous acutely psychiatric patients in Hawaii were sent to Queen's. The only other locked unit was the state hospital with minimal medical capacity. The unit where I wound up working in was called Kekela, which is translated as "Excellence from Heaven." This had two separate units connected. One unit was called Makai, which is translated as "Toward the Sea." This was considered the open unit, which had a regular locked door to the outside. This big steel locked door opened to the other unit where the worst of the worst patients were placed. This unit was called Mauka, which is translated as "Toward the Mountains." Usually, the most dangerous patients went to Mauka, then transferred to Makai when they were closer to baseline—safer patients who were not considered explosive. Sometimes, more than several times, this didn't work out, and we had major takedowns, which was when we required all staff from both units, Makai and Mauka, for takedowns. Both units could get very rowdy! All the staff on both units were considered shared for major takedowns.

So my new life's pathway started. I spent most of my career in this world of insanity. I developed deep feelings for my patients, probably because I remembered when a big chunk of my own pathways was filled with this mental suffering. I spent over nine years at Queen's and under two years in Guam.

The Guam's State Psychiatric Hospital, along with the government of Guam, was very different to Queen's. Guam's care for their mentally ill is very different than America's complete lack of care for their mentally ill people. I was very bored in Guam; I will elaborate on this later. For all the time I spent in Guan, I never had one takedown.

Now that I have finally finished working, I have never forgotten the patients for whom I cared for. Many of these patients were multiple repeaters through the years. In about 1998, I sat down and documented memories of my patients' stories that happened in the Makai and Mauka units. Remember, the normal description of a well-maintained mentally ill person with normal brain functioning capacity from your everyday world would not be in our units. In our unit, there were people born with inherited brain illness or damaged brains from drugs or alcohol or accidental brain damage.

You might see these people standing on a corner, loudly shouting about God, Lord, or the Almighty, professing that they have the direct words to save you. Or you may also see them standing in the street, a person, nude or clothed, hollering and trying to direct traffic. Or a person standing on a box, ranting about returning from the "Galaxies Council" on the "planet of Thear" and how they and they alone can save the planet earth! Also, many of these patients are in prisons and many are called street people, living out of garbage cans, committing small crimes for a roof and food security. Psychotic people off their meds usually get completely irrational and are unable to be safe to themselves or other people.

Helping highly acute psychotic patients to get back to a manageable baseline was my job. Most of my patients lived extremely sad lives and most are not accepted as real human beings! I remember when in my own life I lived that life of always on the fringe of humanity, never quite acceptable to others in my own mind. I had no self-confidence, always felt subjected to smart, normal people. When assessing life's pathways for psychotic people, my heart breaks, because so few ever had a chance at any of life's pathways. I keep repeating this observation over and over because our government keeps ignoring them, just doing nothing, hoping enough of these people will just die suddenly and go away. Today, I see these insane people all over and placed into our prisons where they don't belong. This is a false mindset, and as a country, we must face facts. These people are not dying fast enough—we have to care for them!

Occasionally on our unit, we had sociopathic real killers, some of them with AIDS, trying to kill everybody both on and outside the unit. One sociopathic patient with AIDS, I'll call him Steve, tried to infect everybody by scratching an opened wound on his leg, then with his fingers full of fluid, he scratched unsuspecting persons. Then he would say, "OOPS, sorry. Didn't see you there." One time, as I was applying Steve's dressing to his open leg wound, and he reached out and scratched my arm. I finished taping his wound, went into our medicine room, and vigorously washed my scratches, wondering, "Oh My God, I bet that damn bastard nailed me!" A year later, I found out I had AIDS. I will share more about the full story of Steve later.

Previewing the World of Insanity

Right now, I have a desire to show society what staff have to face every day to care for the whole side of acute psychotic mental illness. Normal, rational people couldn't possibly ever imagine, let alone understand, the true depth of such an illness.

To this day, I can't truly say I totally understand their minds. There were basically two tools we could use to keep our patients and staff safe besides medicine. The first tool was distraction, a simple tool and always available. But this tool wouldn't work usually on the most violent patients. The second tool we had was leather restraints.

With these restraints, we could always safely direct an explosive patient to a safe area, such as their room. By getting some medication into them, they could, within an hour, be back out safely. Of course, there always was one exception. I'll never forget a male patient weighing over three hundred pounds, a former football player, well over six feet tall, whom we nicknamed Rocky, not his real name. Completely psychotic and angry, he slipped out of his waist restraint to which both hands were still attached. Wheeling the strap through the air like a weapon, he slammed it on the tables, furniture, and walls. Then he turned his attention onto every human being in our Mauka unit. His arms were totally free with both straps in his hands, freely moving them in all direction, and his waistband was a buckled weapon!

Everybody started scrambling around the unit. I dove around our unit nursing station desk into the open-door closet behind me. Suddenly, I had three male psych aides pushing me out to where I was standing outside of the door opening and all the males got behind me. Now I was standing on the outside of the doorway staring into Rocky's wild, enraged eyes locking in on my eyes. Rocky stood before the desk while raising his restraints to optimum height for a full capacity strike while staring down at me. I was getting ready to dive to the floor, when a female PA, psychiatric assistant, looking very delicate under her five-foot frame, weighing less than one hundred pounds, walked up and tapped Rocky on his shoulder. Rocky turned his head toward her. She started talking to him, and immediately, his arms started to relax and started to come down. Seeing the relaxed arms coming down, I sprinted around the desk along with the guys in the closet. Joining us were the Makai staff, who had been waiting for a break, already on a dead run, racing down the hall. Collectively, all of us got there within a split second.

We were the first to hit Rocky's midriff and legs, knocking him backward. As we went down, the Makai staff were on his arms and chest. I wound up straddling over Rocky's left upper leg, with both my hands forcing down on his quadriceps with all my strength! Lord! I could feel his muscles moving around; the strength of those muscles was WHOA! His lower right leg broke free. I could barely see his knee coming up and leg kicking out at the staff. The psych aide went flying backward into a wall. Within a matter of seconds, the psych aide jumped up and was back on his legs again, shaking his head. At least seven to eight staff were on top of him. We got his waist restraint out of his hands and reopened the restraint then closed the restraint up and back where it belonged. His wrist restraints were still where they belonged. We got him up quickly and took him back, getting him back to his bed. Then came the Haldol shot. Soon after, he looked like he was settling down, so we loosened up his restraints a little.

After we walked out of the room, I turned to the male staff that had pushed me out of the closet saying, "Okay, guys, I've always heard of 'ladies first,' but that was ridiculous. Don't ever try to be gentlemen again!" The aide that flew into the wall after we got Rocky back to his room had to go down to the emergency room to get checked out.

Over the years, Rocky was a multiple frequent flyer. He was always so apologetic after he got to baseline. At baseline, Rocky was like a gigantic pussycat, warm, cuddly, and very soft spoken. Talk about night and day!

The reason I know that normal people cannot say they understand what working in these units is like is because normal people pushed laws taking away the only major tool we had to create a safe unit! That major tool was leather restraints. Restraints were vilified by normal people who didn't have any knowledge of what they were talking about! The best safety tool we had was leather restraints. We could get a very dangerous patient up out of bed, walking him around with wrist restraints tied to a waist restraint. With this restraint, a patient could never, with their arms, strike out and hit anybody! We could loosen the wrist restraint to eat or take a shower or watch TV. But most importantly, a potentially violent patient could never take a full swing at another patient or staff.

Leather restraints were used many times in my unit. I am an avid defender of restraints! We could do so much more with the patient. We never had to leave them alone in a padded cell. Patients were able to be a part of our unit. They were never alone. When a wound-up patient first walked through the locked doors, we knew immediately they were probably sleep deprived and had been unmerciful in both abusing and neglecting their own bodies. The first order of care for the wild ones would be to get them into restraints, then provide medication, hydration, and sleep. While sleeping, we would decrease the restraints, and if they woke up and needed to get up for any reason, we could use walking restraints and take care of any of their needs, without danger to anybody. I admit that I never worked near any unit with padded cells. I don't have a clue how patients get medicated or their ADLs (activities of daily living) taken care of.

Lord, imagine if they have to have a full team securing them just to use the toilet. Same for any other kind of care—a team of staff or security guards would be required. No single person could just open the door and walk in to talk to them. Patients would have to be so isolated! Then if they get out of isolation before they're ready, they will lack control of their own behavior and start erupting. Then staff, visitors, and patients are going to get hurt. The staff will have to run away or take them down. Then when they take them down, how will they get a fighting, struggling patient up to walk them back to their padded cell? Cops have handcuffs to put a suspect's hands behind their back. What do staff have? Also, there is no place for the other patients to flee or get away from being punched. Unused bathrooms can get crowded very quickly!

All this is because most people who never had to care for severely mentally ill or insane people did a lot of bad-mouthing about how horrible and cruel restraints were. In all the years I worked with severely mentally ill patients, not once did I use or witness any abuse of restraints. No patient was ever harmed because of restraints. Most of the public don't have a clue how dangerous it is to work in a high-acuity unit or to be with a patient completely out of control, which is extremely physically dangerous for both staff and patients! I am sure there has been some abusive use of restraints. However, the same could be said of padded cells! Abuse does not come from the tools but from the person's usage of the tools. Anywhere you have ignorant staff without proper training or the lack good supervisors or administrators that don't care about the staff and their jobs or the patients, you're inviting abuse!

My first eight years at Queen's, I had two wonderful supervisors (bosses): Flo and Barb. They both knew and could work the unit as well as any staff person. My bosses expected the staff to care for and take care of the patients. That was made very clear to us. Anything less than that, we would be out of a job! We were never exposed to any of the hospital's political interactions with our unit. In my last year, hospital politics became the most horrific experience I ever had to go through. Working with psychotic or insane patients seemed so much simpler than working with the psychiatric-ignorant hospital management people!

In addition, I know normal people don't understand the total loss of any rational ability of our high-acuity patients. This was evidenced after I took a full whole quarter of psych in college. I learned very quickly after I walked into the unit. I was absolutely and totally ignorant. I had to learn that my world of reality couldn't fit in a world of insanity. There was not one thing taught to me in psych school that I could use. Talk about being scared. I went out and bought some diapers for myself. That helped me get through the first days while I was being trained. All the years working with staff, nobody ever got personally angry or upset with patients. I had one exception for me, which was Steve. I had angry feelings about Steve, so I never worked with him again. Other staff agreed with me and made sure I was excluded from his care. That was the way we worked together. Always, when we were working, we were not individuals. We were always a team, no matter what personal feelings we may have had. Feelings like that were simply a luxury we couldn't afford. In extreme cases, we made exceptions for care, but never in a takedown. In takedowns, there were no exceptions.

None of us took anything personally about a patient being out of control—punching us, throwing or kicking us into walls, hitting us with chairs, spitting on us, throwing feces or urine on us, or calling us all kinds of names. These patients were hurting at the epitome of losing any rational thought processes or control of their own bodies. We knew that. It was our job to help them, not hurt them. I believe psychotic mental pain is just as bad as or worse than any physical pain and requires the same attention. After some time, many patients getting back on their medications would apologize and feel bad if they did remember correctly how they blew up. We would tell them that's why we're here. Our job is to help you. We understand you were sick and look at you now; you're back on your meds! This was the baseline for them. If we took our unit and compared it to a hospital's medical units, our unit would fall into ICU (intensive care unit), a range at which place medical patients were sent when they're in a life and death crisis.

Welcome to the World of Insanity

∽

I am so grateful and proudly place this job description into my book. Today, Queen's emphasizes in 2022 a very honest job description, which can be found below. The bad guys of my last year didn't win. I felt so relieved. The good guys won (will explain later). This job description is honest and truthful. I couldn't ask for anything more. Here I want to say thank-you to all the forces that saved our Kekela unit to the high standard of truth!

Typical Working Conditions

Exposure to body fluids, blood products, and communicable diseases. Work environment is highly stressful, fast-paced, and hectic. Assignment to inpatient adult psych areas and family treatment center includes occasionally accompanying patients outdoors. Management of confused or disoriented and combative patients may involve tasks which may compromise physical safety.

The next pages are my written patient experiences straight from Queen's Hospital Psychiatric Unit. I wrote these memories in about 1997–1998 after leaving work. Welcome!

I arrived at Queen's Hospital Kekela Unit in 1984 as a brand-new graduate—albeit a thirty-nine-year-old super mom. My Super Mom years were over! I was fresh out of school. I obtained a position in the acute psychiatric unit (Kekela) of Honolulu's historically prestigious Queen's Hospital. This was Hawaii's answer to the rest of the state's largest teaching county hospitals and was mandated to provide medical care for the poor Hawaiian people. My only thought was "At last, a job." And to think I had been worried about being bored! Life really is full of surprises, and I was due for quite a few. Throughout my career, learning would become a never-ending job, and survival would become a daily battle. Not one day was I ever bored.

What I really knew about psychiatric patients was nothing. School had taught us the concepts about theoretical psych nursing care. However, having a tall, big male patient stick his face within one inch of your face, his eyes boring into yours, and his fingers clenching your windpipe while saying, "Bitch, get me a cigarette right now," or "I'm going to cut you up into little pieces and feed you to my dog!" This was a whole different learning curve. As urine was running into my diaper, the patient got his cigarette right now, and I kept thinking, *Dog? What dog? We don't allow dogs on the unit.* There was so much confusion in my mind that I kept trying to fit what had been the real world into a world where reality was nonexistent. One of the first evenings during my orientation, I felt like I had gone fifteen rounds with psychotic reality and lost. I was on the Mauka's locked psychiatric unit with nineteen patients, two nurses, and four psychiatric assistants (PAs.)

One of my first nights, I was hurrying down the hall toward a yelling patient, who was screaming that she was being raped. Another patient was screaming something in her room. As I was racing toward all the hollering, I heard, "Help, please help me." I rushed into the room and saw Kitty, our psychiatric assistant (PA), grabbing a male patient's penis. I was horrified. I knew what she was doing. After all, I'd heard all those stories about how we mistreat psychiatric patients. "Kitty, let go of Tim's privates right now!"

Kitty's disgust was evident. "Ginger, Tim's trying to pull his penis off!"

I hollered back, "Kitty, men don't do that. It's too painful!"

Kitty's anger was replaced with disgust. "Okay, watch." Kitty released, and Tim made one quick grab for his penis and yanked it hard. I watched stunned. My only instinctive reaction was "I've never seen a male pull his penis out that far. Ouch!"

Both Kitty and I jumped in and grabbed Tim's hands. The fight was on. Our hands became a scrambled mess of pubic hair, sweat, and urine. At one point, Kitty went up and over Tim as he got his right hand into her hair and yanked hard, bashing her head into the wall by his bed. I wound up crossways over Tim, trying to protect his extended penis with his left hand and trying to pull at his right hand to release Kitty's hair. During the whole fight, Tim was screaming something about the devil's instrument and being cursed. I'm guessing here, but it sounded to me like he had, for him, an "evil" affair with another woman. Within seconds, seeming like hours, full staff response came on a run. One male PA was kicked across the room as he approached the bed and was slammed into the wall like a lightweight football.

Another nurse raced in and gave him a shot of Haldol. With enough staff, we finally restrained Tim's hands and feet. After Tim was fully restrained, which meant hands and ankles were in leather cuffs, after kicking two more staff, a leather belt waist was placed around his waist so that finally Tim was fully anchored to the bed. As I walked out of the room, I could feel my hands burning from the scratches combined with body fluids. I looked at Kitty with the lump on her head swelling.

We had just gotten Tim settled down, when in walked his wife and his mother. They took one look at Tim and demanded to know why he was in restraints. They saw Tim, quiet by now, and gave me the soon-to-be well-learned lecture on how cruel we were—how uncaring we were to this poor helpless human being. This poor son, this poor husband, so loved by them, so abused by us. I just looked at them briefly, bit my tongue, and made the decision that Tim's wife would never learn from me about his potential affair. Tim was psychotic from one too many runs to the angel dust (PCP) though, and this family were the only ones to take care of him over the years to come. Tim had, through drug use, not only lost his reality but also lost some of his motor functions. For example, the staff had to sit him down just to eat a meal. He'd grab his food and smash it into his face. He'd lost the concept of silverware and chewing. Same with bathing, Tim would stand in a shower but played like a child. Tim had no concept of using a washcloth and washing. We learned, after many showers with Tim, that the staff would come out whistle clean and Tim would come out trying to swing, within the limits of his waist restraints. Oh, yeah, his family deserved a lot of consideration. They were facing years of long hard labor, which would be measured in inches not yards.

Immediately upon leaving the room, I profusely apologized to Kitty, who's response was "Well, Ginger, it takes time. We've all had to learn!" I managed to get my hands washed just in time to respond to a female patient, Ellen. Ellen was screaming. Actually, she had been screaming most of the time we were taking care of Tim. The other patients were getting agitated with all the screaming.

Okay, Tim's crisis is done. Now over to Ellen's room, I heard, "Get me a doctor! My water broke, the baby's coming…" I looked at Ellen, pulling the sheet back. She was a very large woman, and I saw a pool of fluid. She was groaning now and saying her water had broken, and she had to start pushing the baby out. I ran back to the nurses' station and told Marty, the charge nurse, to get a doctor. I was scared and frantic. Ellen was having her baby now. Marty stood calmly looking at me and asked, "Ginger, what is Ellen's age and diagnosis?"

I attempted to focus my eyes on Marty while practically shouting, "Who cares? Ellen is having a baby, and I don't know how to deliver one."

Marty started laughing. "Ginger, Ellen is fifty-four years old and delusional. She isn't having a baby. She needs help with her delusion." Oh, yeah, I remember. *Delusion*, that was the word which I kept mixing up with *illusion*.

Going back to Ellen, who was still screaming that she was having a baby, I kept trying to calm her down. For the life of me, I simply could not convince Ellen she wasn't having a baby, and I couldn't think how to distract her. My mind was totally in overload, thoughts racing. "Never argue with a delusional person. Don't verbally engage the delusional system. Keep reorienting the patient to reality." What was obvious was Ellen hadn't gone very far in school. She didn't know the rules. Like wings of angels, the staff came and rescued me. They told her she needed a shower, and the bed had to be cleaned up. She stopped shouting and said okay. So Ellen got up and was taken to the shower, which briefly distracted her, while I went and got the bed made.

Later on that evening, we went through the whole process again. But for the moment, I had been saved by staff distraction. I, at that time, couldn't think of distractions. By the end of my shift, I gave up. I delivered Ellen's delusional baby. At that point, I couldn't have cared less how the next shift was going to produce Ellen's baby for holding and feeding. No need to worry about the baby. I found out the next night, Ellen didn't want to know anything about her baby as her delusion began and ended with having the baby! All of Ellen's screaming had set the unit off. Talk about a domino effect in which no man is an island, and suddenly, nine out of the nineteen patients were getting loud and angry. The problem was not even half of the patients were rational enough to understand why they felt upset. They were just upset.

The same patient that had been screaming about being raped was still screaming at a PA standing about ten feet away from her, "Get your penis out of me. Help. Help me, I'm being raped!" I grabbed her arm and got her to her room, where she started making scratching-like motions with her feet on the floor, folded her hands under her armpits, and began flapping her elbows and started squawking like a rooster. Marty, who had remained calm throughout this whole episode, asked, "Ginger, can you think of anything that might help the patients?"

I tried to focus my eyes on Marty's face, looking for a clue, my mind blank. "No, nothing comes to mind."

The only thought now was *Oh! Oh! Everybody knows I'm not a nurse. I'm going to lose my job. What lesson was it, I've forgotten?*

Marty suggested, "Ginger, why don't you see if there are any medications ordered for the patients that might help them calm down?"

Instinctively, this sounded right, but in school, we were taught to try everything else before we tried medication. As I stood transfixed by all the screaming and noise, I was desperate. "To hell with school. Where is the medication book?"

Subduing the Storm

I left work that night thinking, *Did I say psych was boring?* I felt like such a failure. I had jumped to all the wrong conclusions about my coworkers and had dumped the very tenets of my schooling. Reality in an insane world is very different from anything else I had ever experienced in my life. I knew one thing. I was on a very steep learning curve, and I'd better learn quickly. Over the next years, learning how to truly care for mentally ill patients became a never-ending challenge. When you learn about mentally ill people, you also learn about being able to trust your instincts and understanding all the nuances of many different overt and subtle human behaviors. Working in a locked psych unit reminds me of being in a storm during a hot summer's evening in Kansas, with each patient playing his or her own part of the storm. Some are like the quiet, sultry heaviness, anticipating their own preludes for what's to come. Some are like lightning snapping across the sky—frighteningly deadly. Some are close enough with terrifying, explosive, and thundering booms, scaring the life out of you just in percussion. Yet some are still hiding in the boiling clouds—alive and waiting for the final ingredient to fulfill the full violent climax of the storm.

Within our four walls, our job is to subdue the storm. Medication and communication become a lifeline to patients. One of my elderly mentors, Karyl, taught me medicating a patient is like listening to music. You have to hear and respond before the music is completed, building to a crescendo. For communication, a nurse needs to be able to understand what their patient's nonreality is and deal with that in real reality. A lifetime of challenge, never to be truly mastered by any one person; but always, when you walk away from a patient, you know you have left them with their dignity. Karyl also taught me to always stay focused on the patient and what I was doing to the patient. "Ginger, you'll never get in trouble or go wrong if you train yourself to focus on the patient."

Remembering one of my early working days in Mauka, I came out of an area where there was a set of three patient rooms and a bathroom with a short hallway ending up at a longer and very wide hallway, which led from the steel locked door up to the unit's nursing station. The steel doors were at the opposite end of the long, wide hallway for the unit. This was a much bigger hallway, having sliding doors leading to the patio on one side, and on the other side there was a bathtub room, along with our unit room for shift report. I was down working with a patient, and I came out of the room and turned into the wide hallway seeing a male patient, lean and very tall, who I didn't recognize. He started to walk down the hallway from the nurses' station. His arms were extended straight out. He just kept walking right at me, staring straight at me.

When I was about halfway down the hallway, I stopped and started to back up. I could see the nurses' station with a couple of staff looking at me along with Marty. I hollered to them for help. They just stood there not saying a word. He just kept coming at me. I just kept backing up and looking and hollering for the staff. He was getting close, and I was running out of hallway. Marty finally hollered down to me, "Ginger! Just stand still." Terrified now, my mind was exploding with, *Why aren't they helping me? What did I do wrong? They aren't going to help me!* The patient came up to me, clamped his arms around my body, and lifted me up off the floor. With my head held back inches away from his face, he stared into my eyes and said,

"Hello, my name is John." I replied with, "Hi, my name is Ginger." Then he put me back onto the floor and walked off.

I was shaking, my mind was a jumbled racing mess. I saw the patio doors and just went out, sat down, and lit up a cigarette. After a while, a couple of staff came out and sat down with me. "Ginger, are you okay?"

I said, "No. I don't know what to think. You guys just left me."

By now I was crying. "Oh, Ginger," my staff said. "We knew him. He's one of the gentlest people we have ever had in this unit. We knew he wasn't going to hurt you!"

I told them, "Well, I'm glad you guys knew that. I didn't. All I knew was I was alone. I couldn't think what I had done wrong, that you guys would let me get hurt."

Staff's response was "Oh, no, no, you didn't do anything wrong. Ginger, we just thought it was a joke. We're always there for each other. Always! Please forgive us. It was a bad joke. That's obvious." They went back inside. Then the whole staff came out.

We had a great talk. I calmed down and even started laughing. I was curious why he was in our unit and not over on Makai. They told me he lost his home and needed placement, so his psychiatrist tried to get him a bed on Makai, but they were full. So he got sent to us on Mauka.

So went work. At times it was very lonely, because the psych world was difficult to share with others. Also, we developed a very dark sense of humor. For people outside our working community, the humor wasn't funny. So many of our patients' lives were nothing more than a great tragedy. However, the staff has to work off a lot of physical and verbal abuse. Humor is one way. Most of our humor was directed at ourselves and our own mental status.

Shame on Me

Dan was always one of my favorite people to tease. Dan RN had been a nurse at Kekela for many years before me. He had one patient, Jess, who wasn't going to rest until he got rid of Dan. Jess was convinced Dan had a computer in his head and was the devil incarnate. Dan, according to Jess, also spent all his time reading that computer. One day, Dan was sitting in the day area writing, when Jess vaulted across the room and knocked Dan out with a haymaker punch. Ever since then, Dan refused to be anywhere near Jess.

So when Dan was busy and a little distracted, we would pretend to answer the phone and get information on a patient down in ER being admitted to the unit. We would look over at Dan and tell him he was up for a new admission. He would say, "Okay. Who?" We would casually say, "Jess!" Geez! It was fun to watch Dan's face turn to full on panic. Dan would get just beside himself, horrified. That worked for us. Never missed a good laugh on that one. Dan was laughing with us after we told him we were teasing him. We mostly all had a good sense of humor, and Dan took his turns with any of us. Also, Dan had his own ideas of getting back at me, like posting stickers on my back with disgusting humor!

Around the 1990s, nurses came up against the concepts of gender issues in the workplace. Up until then, nurses were primarily females, and nobody thought about working with men. Approximately 90 percent of our nurses were females, and out of the 10 percent males, 80 percent of those male RNs were in administrative positions. So sexism among the nurses had never really been defined. Around the '90s, that changed dramatically, with an increase of male nurses. Sexism on the unit was about to be defined, or not, never to be resolved. Defining male, female nursing roles and the differences of what was okay or not okay was never resolved in my time!

I remember one particular day, I was showering an elderly demented gentleman, who also had what appeared to me to be an inguinal hernia. Every time he stood up, his testicles dropped about halfway to his knees. Regardless, he needed a shower, so here I was in a running shower, trying to wash his low swinging testicles and all the skin folds—so many folds needed washing. Along with the fact the folds wouldn't open, it was like they were glued together, all this time he was slapping me on the top of my head, hollering, "Quit fooling around with me!"

A male PA came to the door and asked, "How's your shower going, Ginger? We thought we'd better check. The unit thinks you're in there raping him."

Soaked to the skin, I looked at the PA and replied, "My shower is going just great, and if you don't quit smirking, I'm going to do something mean and ugly to your testicles."

Then the PA offered to take over as I had a phone call. When I answered the phone, it was Dan RN on the open unit. "Ginger, I have an order to put in a urine catheter on my patient Jane. We don't have any female nurses over here right now. So could you come over and do the catheter?"

I naturally asked, "Why?"

Dan immediately said, "Oh, I can't do that."

"What do you mean you can't do that?" I responded.

"Well, I'm not comfortable violating my patient's modesty," said Dan.

Again, I responded, "What the hell do you mean violate your female patient's modesty? I've been grabbing males' penises for years and sinking tubes in them. Does your patient mind? Ask, Dan. If I remember correctly, this patient has been catatonic for days? If you can get a response out of her while inserting the catheter, you've made great headway." I quickly added, "If she starts screaming at you, then I'll come over!" Then I slammed the phone down. As I looked up, the staff were wide-eyed and laughing. For weeks, that was the joke of the unit.

The next day, in my report, I told my staff, "I couldn't do a good job yesterday, cleaning the demented gentleman's testicles. He needs a bath as his testicle folds were practically glued together. His testicles need to be soaked and gently open the folds. I am afraid there might be sores in there. If you're cleaning them and they start to bleed, come get me." The staff responded they could do it, and they did it, no blood.

For the male staff, I do sympathize with them. The male nurses and male staff don't get a fair shake. Sometimes a few of the female nurses who had a very heavy or particularly dangerous patient would say, "Oh, I couldn't do that. He's too heavy," or "He might hit me." We had many a royal battle and many laughs at ourselves over what was "appropriate." I often thought if we ever do evolve to a truly unisex mentality type world, we are going to lose a lot of our current humor. Also, for the male staff, it was always harder for them. Women patients screaming that a male touched them inappropriately always brought about a dramatic hunt for the sexually perverted male staff stalking and preying on the innocent female. Whereas for female staff, the reverse was true. A male patient screaming that a female had violated him just didn't carry the same weight and response.

One of my first experiences along the lines of dealing with an opposite sex patient who was sexually preoccupied was Mr. Tang. Mr. Tang was sixty-eight years old. He was physically about as repulsive as one could get. The man was filthy. He had fingernails very long and filthy dirty. He was toothless and made smacking sounds. He had covered himself in his own feces. In the report, we were told Mr. Tang had attacked several people when he arrived in the unit today and was in restraints. The day nurses had given him medication to try to calm him down and asked if maybe our shift could get him cleaned up. Well, of course we could. I sent staff down to do just that. Two minutes later, staff came back and informed me they would not be doing anything with Mr. Tang until I gave him some more medication.

Well, I just had to go see this for myself. After all, the man only weighed about eighty-nine pounds. I, in my moment of glorious self-righteousness, walked into Mr. Tang's room. See, there was Mr. Tang lying peacefully in his bed. I walked right up to his bed. His eyes were closed, and I leaned over and quietly asked him how he was feeling. My eyes didn't even have a chance to blink. Mr. Tang's hands grabbed my head and slammed it down into his body that was smeared with feces and screamed, "I know what you want. You just want to fuck me! That's what you all want to do. So fuck me!"

Staff immediately tried to get my head released. Thank heavens the staff, much smarter than I had been, had followed me and were standing outside the door waiting. By the time I was able to stand upright, I gave my staff the look and said as primly as I could, "I think Mr. Tang needs more medication."

One male PA kindly put his arm around me and said supportively, "Ginger, I realize Mr. Tang wasn't your type." My staff deserved an apology and a thank-you for saving me, and I deserved the kidding about my behavior! I stood in the bathroom for at least ten minutes trying to get cleaned up, especially my nostrils. Staring into the bathroom mirror, I swore to myself, "The next time I get that self-righteous feeling, I'm going to ask somebody to come up and slap me." I told the staff it was hard for me to admit, but they needed to know that with deep regret, I had fallen into an arrogant pit and deserved any self-contempt toward me. "Well, give it back to me. I so deserve it!"

It took me days to stop smelling Mr. Tang. For the rest of his stay, Mr. Tang kept telling all the other patients that I had raped him. Inversely, if this had happened to a comale staff with a female patient, which happens more for the guys then the gals, the whole situation would have been treated as a potential female patient abuse by a male staff—sad but true. Since it was a female staff to male patient, for a week all I heard was "Ginger, we really admire you. The way you resisted that hunk of male flesh. I just don't know if I would have had the strength to resist such a specimen. Tee-hee!"

Male or female patients produced a whole new set of rules. The rule we had clung to was "men violate women." Not the other way around. Yet women do violate men, just in different ways. Women don't usually physically throw men to the ground and jump on them. Yet, very effectively, a woman will seductively use emotional and physically blackmail to gain control over a male.

Sandy was one very sexually preoccupied female patient. By the time she was discharged, she must have attacked at least four male patients. They didn't know what hit them. One of the male patients was Jerry. I had known Jerry for years. After we caught him having sexual intercourse with Sandy, I asked him how it had happened. Jerry said she kept rubbing up against him all day and trying to fondle his privates. "I didn't know what to do. She just kept telling me she wanted me. Before the change of shift, she had come to my room, took off her clothes, and pushed me to the bed. I just kept saying, 'We can't be doing this, I don't know if I can get it up.' She got mad and started hitting me and saying she'd tell the staff I was raping her. I was scared. So I did it."

Jerry felt terrible. He was, after all, over six feet tall weighing about 260 pounds, and Sandy was about just over five feet weighing about 120 pounds. He just kept saying nobody would believe him if she hollered rape. I told Jerry that I had known him for so many years and realized he would never try to molest or hurt a woman. He wasn't prepared for the Sandys of the world. The results were almost always the same. Any sexual contact talk brought about for the males, "Shame on you," and a lot of, "Oh, your poor baby," for the females with counseling if needed. I never did see rape counseling for a male patient unless he had claimed sexual rape by a male patient. However, Sandy did push that point pretty far. After her third victim, some of the staff were trying to warn the males. Yet that old rule of confidentiality was getting in the way.

Nobody ever developed a plan for dealing with sexual issues between patients or for staff dealing with patients of the opposite sex. I can still hear all the sexual issues from the 1990s being debated today, as if dealing with gender differences was a newly invented concept. I have learned that staff have to be around long enough to develop awareness of this kind of problem and its resolution. In other words, the staff needs experience.

Tara was a stripper and financially was doing quite well. After a couple hours of being in the unit, her real issue came out. Tara was pregnant. Problem was she was involved with two men. I'll call the gentlemen in Tara's life Mr. X and Mr. Y. Well, if Mr. Y was the father, she would be happy to have the baby and get married. Mr. Y was monetarily very well off. Now if the father of her baby was Mr. X, she wanted to have an abortion, without Mr. Y's knowledge. Then she would be depressed and get Mr. Y to support her emotionally through her "miscarriage." Also, Tara liked her cocaine and heroin. Soon she was moving into withdrawals, which also led to many staff getting punched as Tara threw her temper tantrums.

Our difficulty was trying to keep Mr. X and Mr. Y apart and their identities straight. Between us, mixing up Mr. X and Mr. Y led to Tara's explosions. Tara finally decided she wanted to get out of the unit and go back to her cocaine and her old figure after the abortion. So Tara demanded an abortion. Then the day after the abortion, Tara, with her eyes full of tears, told Mr. Y that we had pressured her into an abortion. She never on her own would have ever given up a child that was theirs. I listened to her go on and on for hours about how abused she was. She forgot to tell him the part about the cruelest thing we did to her, which was not let her have as many drugs as she was demanding! We explained to her that taking a lot of narcotic drugs during a pregnancy wasn't healthy for an unborn baby. She did eventually get herself linked up with foolish old Mr. Y. Believe me, love can be extraordinarily blind. For all of us, we just became the recipients of a lot of her physical and verbal lashing out. She was a slapper toward both staff and patients. With a pregnant woman, there is no way you can physically restrain her. We couldn't medicate her enough to suit her extensive drug habit. Communication became an impossible walk on eggshells.

One for the Team

Each member of staff has their own ability to understand any psychotic illness. As staff, we had to learn our own human biases without too much expecting to fully overcome them. At least we should know our human biases, so we could diminish personalizing our interaction with patients. We would usually try with difficult patients, either to rotate or to look at which one of us could work best with different patients.

I always looked with great admiration at the psychiatrists who would stay year after year working with the same patients, demanding every desire be met. That kind of dedication took an extraordinary amount of patience, energy, and stamina. Not to mention this dedication to duty was still carried out when one of the psychiatrist's particularly difficult patients would be admitted into the unit.

We were an unusual psych unit because we also took care of some medically compromised patients along with a psychotic diagnosis. So at any given moment, we not only had patients around the unit with hostile explosive behavior but we also had patients with IVs, pre- or post-surgery, geriatrics, OB, and so on.

Then Terry pops into my mind. She had been on Lithium for a long time but hadn't been getting her lab level drawn or taking enough fluid. The result was Terry developed a megacolon, and it ruptured. So when Terry came into the unit, she was full-blown manic and had a colostomy bag attached to her bowel for fecal collection. For about two months, Terry was to our unit like a two-hundred-megaton energy boost. No way could we keep the colostomy bag on her. She was squirting everybody with her feces. At least two times a day, we had to retrieve another patient's flower petals, small objects, pencils, food, and utensils from her exposed stoma, the hole in the bowel, where the colostomy bag attaches. Finally, her psychiatrist was able to get one of the surgeons to perform a resection of her colon and sew her intestines back together. This was actually quite a feat. Terry didn't have insurance, and Medicaid perceived the operation as unnecessary. Staff thought it would be really helpful for Terry to have colostomy surgery. She couldn't take care of it. We thought she should have her intestine put back together!

Days before Terry's surgery, we had to work out an extensive plan for her pre- and post-surgery. We had a couple of heated arguments, but we pulled together and worked hard for the plan! Terry didn't have the capacity to help in any way. We had to run multiple bottles of fluid through her digestive system. Terry wound up restrained and sedated for this. So we couldn't leave her side for this procedure. On the day of surgery, staff took Terry down to surgery. In less than half an hour, Terry was on her way back up. The surgeon declared Terry wasn't cleaned out enough and refused to do the surgery! Back up on the unit, we all thought, *Oh, shit! We have to go through all the prep again!*

I will add that in my personal life, I had made friends with one of the operating room nurses. Sharon became my best friend for many years. She had a long history of OR nursing at Queen's. I talked to Sharon about this patient. She knew the surgeon and told me, "Ginger, he didn't want to do the surgery. He says that when he doesn't want to do the surgery. Don't worry. Bring her down again. I'll take care of her!"

So we did the prep again, and this time, I took Terry down to surgery. The assigned OR nurse looked at her operation consent and told Terry she was there for a colostomy reversal. Terry said, "Oh, no, I'm here for plastic surgery." The OR nurse looked at me and said, "This patient doesn't understand her surgery. She can't have this surgery until she fully understands it." I wanted to scream! For two months, we had been cleaning up Terry's foul-smelling feces and trying to teach her what was happening to her body. I told the nurse that Terry was delusional at times, but she had clear moments and understood the surgery.

At that moment, Sharon came through the doors. Just like a princess on her white steed, Sharon, while giving me a wink, said, "I'm taking over on this patient."

The other nurse was sputtering, "But you can't! She doesn't even know what surgery she's having!"

Sharon just gave her look and said, "The surgeon is on his way into the room. Let's go."

Off went Terry and Sharon. I felt a big sigh of relief. Terry did get better on the med surge floor after surgery and, except for a scar, had a functioning digestive system.

Later Sharon told me, "The surgeon started with she was not cleaned out well enough." Sharon said that she told him in no uncertain terms that she was cleaned out well enough, and this surgery will be taking place now!

I hollered, "Yeah, one for the team!"

We heard years later that Terry was found on the freeway in her parked car. The windows were all rolled up. The sun was hot, and the inside of the car was steaming. Terry was pulled out of her car barely alive. Terry died in the ER from heat exhaustion.

There was life outside of the unit. But after years of existing in a workplace where reality was so altered, my personal thoughts of outside and inside the psychiatric unit couldn't be kept separate. One day, I went with my mother to a symphony preview. To this day, I can't forget the shock of realizing the differences between what people have. The preview was held in a home so lavish. There was a big fountain inside the home. The square footage must have been over multiples of a thousand feet. Thick carpets and all kinds of exclusive artwork were everywhere. The people were very nice. They most certainly enjoyed all the beauty of the home and the music and really fancy pupu (fancy appetizers) to eat. Five hours later, I was back to work sitting with some patients in light drizzling rain and a walled unit patio watching them smoke.

Three patients, in the throes of varying degrees of psychosis with schizophrenia, were huddled together. These three patients, who one hour earlier were fighting, were now three patients sharing their last cigarette. One would puff and pass it off to the other. The one cigarette was all they had left. Their feet had been without shoes for a long time. I could see the thick calluses and the gaping cracks with some dried blood on the soles of one patient's feet. Their teeth were rotten and missing. Legs and arms full of scars and old wounds. Clothing faded and tattered. I had cared for these same patients for years. I sat down with them and shared my pack of cigarettes. I knew two of these patients. They had just come in a couple days ago. One was going around slapping people in the face while hollering at them. We put her in walking restraints for her own safety. The other patient was shaking and crying a lot, needing a lot of tender care. Now all three were pretty much close to baseline and ready to go over to Makai, then back to the streets!

They never really got better. We called these kind of patients revolving-door patients. Get them better, throw them back out on the streets, and back in they'd bounce, until their Medicaid hospital days limit for the year ran out. Now most of the time they just tried to survive. There was no place for them, no home, no beautiful music, and no hope. Not all but most lived out a life of desperation that was beyond anything imaginable to the majority of people or me! My mind just flew back to the opulence I had just experienced that afternoon. Suddenly, I felt a very powerful wave of gut-wrenching revulsion; the division was so stark, so unfair! Yet in our unit, the vast division exists, every day, totally ignored human beings, without any hope!

My thoughts expanded to all the patients. One of my rotating patients was a really cute young man named Charley. Fondly thinking of Charley, devastated by schizophrenia, he was constantly running to the phone. He would claim this was a phone call from his girlfriend and talk to her about how much he loved her, and she would tell him how much she loved him. They carried on about when they would get married, argued about how many children they'd have…

The other patients sometimes would get furious with Charley. I saw one patient get so angry with Charley monopolizing the phone. The patient ripped the phone out of the wall and threw it at Charley. Everybody knew Charley was talking to a dead phone. He didn't have any girlfriend. He didn't have anyone. This unit and his psychiatrist of longstanding were the closest thing to home and family that Charley would ever have. His psychiatrist told us a few months later that Charley just couldn't let go of wanting to be like mentally healthy people. Charley hung himself in a city park and some of us cried for that young man and felt the hopelessness of his life. He just wanted to be loved and have a life!

Tragic Dump Jobs

―――∞―――

In the day area, Mr. Aguayo was sitting in a wheelchair with a soft restraint (made of cloth). Mr. Aguayo was what we called a dump job. He was an old man with dementia. For us, same old story: kids or family were tired, worn out, fed up, who knows why, and would take a parent or grandparent to the emergency room, dump the patient off, and take off in their car. By the time ER people could get on top of what was happening, all they could see were taillights as the car raced away. So here sits the patient in the ER while staff are trying to get somebody to come get him. Well, usually what happened was the patient got turfed to wherever there was a bed. If in the ER, the patient was demented with agitation or assaultive behavior, they would be turfed up to Makai. Mixing a fragile and elderly demented person in a unit with drug-crazed sociopath personalities and psychotic people was not always healthy for the elderly.

Mr. Aguayo had earlier gone up to a patient and slapped her. He wouldn't stay in the confinement of his room. He kept wandering everywhere. Finally, after dragging him out of a male patient's room where he had tried to crawl into bed with a paranoid schizophrenic, we decided he had to be contained. We put him in a wheelchair with a waist restraint. He was going to get himself killed.

After several days, his preacher and granddaughter came to see him. They didn't want to take him home but were very upset to see him in a wheelchair and waist restrained. I could understand that. But no way would Mr. Aguayo survive being in the unit without getting critically hurt. Later I learned the preacher and granddaughter filed complaints with the health department about the waist restraint. This caused a certain amount of flurry, but bottom line was he didn't belong in a psych unit, and there wasn't any place or anybody who wanted him. Sometimes I wish we had an animal humane society for humans.

Reminds me even more of one eighty-year-old lady who had been brought into the unit under similar circumstances several years ago, and we didn't restrain her. Her son had been totally against having his mother restrained in any fashion. So she fell out of bed and wound up with a broken hip. Her family sued and the hospital paid. Last year, she was back in again, and we caught her son on top of her bed trying to push her out of the bed. Guess they had run out of money. It was a good thing some of us had been around long enough to remember how the game was played.

Theresa, a transgender, had for years been coming into the unit depressed. Now Theresa had totally broken from reality. She, formally he, was very beautiful. She had actually done some modeling. After a horrific assault, she was sent down to our unit after surgery and medical unit care. We had very little information on the assault but heard a couple of depraved men, for fun, had decided to destroy her. They had taken Theresa and shredded her anus repeatedly with some kind of metal object. How can this happen? Are there no boundaries for man's inhumanity to man? Theresa now thought she was connected to another planet and empowered by some space energy. She couldn't respond to requests. Theresa would just fall apart in tears. Theresa never in her history in the unit had severe acute psychotic issues. Her mental illness was mainly around depression.

Our staff was horrified at what had happened to Theresa, along with our auxiliary support groups, the social workers. The whole unit pitched in to help Theresa. Social workers found a small support group for Theresa. They came to the unit and worked with her. Staff just showered her with love and attention. Gradually, she came back. I remember the day she left the unit. Everybody that could have been there was there. The social workers brought a goodbye gift of tea (which she loved) and her supper for the night. They made sure her cab took her home. They also made arrangements with the support group for somebody to come later in the day and the next day to visit and check on her. We had already passed the hat around and gave her seventy-five dollars as she walked out the door. She gave all of us big hugs, which we returned. Many of us were in tears.

The multiple phone calls, all hours of the day and night, to the psychiatrist came from the exasperated nurses dealing with their difficult patients. At Kekela, we had up to seventy-five different psychiatrists, with a variety of different care styles for their patients. We could professionally deal with the same diagnosis and a variety of differing needed cares!

One patient I had difficulty understanding was Marie. She was a swallower. She'd swallow anything she could lay her hands on. On one admission, we thought she might be trying to tell us something. The X-rays came back, showing in her stomach a small light bulb, batteries, coins, keys, and fish lures. We asked her if she needed anything else for her fishing trip. Time and again, we would have Marie and one staff person together for as long as possible to keep her from grabbing and swallowing, but we didn't have the staffing for a total twenty-four-hour one-to-one care. Then Marie would say, "I'm okay now." That was usually a lie, and we would have to go through several rounds of swallowing before she really meant it.

Marie was usually fairly safe with what she swallowed and would pick objects that would pass through or could be surgically removed. Needless to say, the medical staff knew her well and would usually be furious with her. One night, she made a major mistake. With staff thinking and hoping—"I'm okay now," she said—she was placed on the open unit, which also had a locked door. She managed to slip out and over to another part of the hospital. While there, she drank isopropyl rubbing alcohol. When Marie got back to the unit, we had gotten a call from the other unit, and the nurse told the Makai nurse that Marie had drunk rubbing alcohol.

A nurse called Marie's psychiatrist, and the decision was made to transfer Marie back to Mauka, the locked unit. When I was notified, I went ballistic. Two years earlier, I had lost a thirteen-year-old girl with complications from drinking rubbing alcohol in a suicide pact with another teenage friend. The poor girl was terrified when she realized she wasn't going to make it. That young girl died later that night! Now I went into full emergency mode. I called down to the ER for a doctor.

We had an emergency! They got Marie up to the ICU and ran a complete IV flush through her. Marie was nearly lost over that stunt. I don't know how or what they did that could have possibly helped her, but she never came back. She survived and was discharged. It was the RN who had made sure we were alerted to what was swallowed and the danger! All I can say for the RN that saved her life, hat's off to you. You saved her life.

With their overwhelming need to cut themselves, self-mutilators were also difficult to understand. Trudy had been mutilating herself for years. When she came in, we had to check every orifice she had. Over the years, we had found one-sided razor blades in her hair, vagina, rectum, inside her buttock cheeks. She'd always just kept getting better at hiding her cutting stash. After a couple of days in the unit, she'd show us her fresh new "owee" and carefully explained to us what we had missed. We'd just shake our heads. Most of us really didn't want to play the game and told her so. We wanted to play, "How can we help you not want to self-mutilate yourself?"

So went work. At times it was very lonely, because the psych world was difficult to share with others. As I've said, we developed a rather dark sense of humor, but it fit us and the world in which we worked. For people outside our working community, the humor wasn't funny. For many of our patients, life was nothing more than a great tragedy. However, staff had to work off a lot of physical and verbal abuse. Humor was one way of doing that. Most of our humor was directed at our own drained mental status.

Angel, one of our nurses, brought about that kind of dark humor. Angel was a slender middle-aged woman. Like many of us, she had gone through the super mom years, had a Peter Pan husband, and was facing years of being divorced and alone. A few of us had dubbed this psychological stage of life, "Penis envy with vaginal neglect." So what do you do? Accept being alone or try to compete with twenty-year-old girls? Well, Angel's style was to recreate her twenties in her forties. Short skirts and loose revealing tops were Angel's work uniform.

Translated to staff, that meant, "Don't ask me to bend over, or if I can't wow the patient with my sexuality, I'll go sit at the nursing station and talk to everybody." In other words, she wasn't available for any physical work. On one shift, all staff were called to a fighting patient. As we ran past Angel, noting she was standing well out of harm's way, she was pointing with her right finger to the room. Angel, with her left hand on her hip, was accentuating her rather flat chest as it rose up and down, giving us the signal, "I am here for you sexually, but am not about to be hit!" When we were running past her and into the room, we knowingly glanced at each other. We could see Angel was not happy as Mr. Smith had not correctly responded to her sexual charms.

So about six of us tackled a male patient who had a female staff in a headlock and was screaming, "Come near me and I'll snap her neck." As we were restraining Mr. Smith on the floor, in bounced Angel, and with one knee on the patient, she placed her other knee in the middle of the patient's rear. Suddenly, all of us lost the whole focus of restraining the patient, and our eyes were wide with disbelief looking down or looking up, depending on which end of the patient you were on, Angel was totally in full view, from her nipples to her Victoria's Secret panties. Our mouths gaped. We looked at each other. We could see each other's faces turning blue, fighting for control to not burst into laughter. Somehow, we finished restraining, while Angel kept swishing her near-exposed rear and chest around in our faces.

We did it. We got out of the room. Laughing so hard, one male PA tripped and fell on the floor. Angel came out of the room, face straight and chin jutting out. "What's going on? What's so funny? Do you think what happened to that poor man was funny? I don't think that was one bit funny."

We just kept looking at each other, laughing even harder, hoping the other guy would tell Angel what had really happened. Finally, one of the older male staff took Angel aside and told Angel that there was way too much of Angel showing and not enough clothing.

Angel just seemed to bring about a lot of dark humorous thoughts in dire circumstances. Quite a few of us realized she just didn't quite get it. For Angel, every patient that could speak rationally, she would superimpose a given diagnosis for the patients' tragic childhoods, which always included lots of sexual abuse. We finally decided she must have been sexually abused as a child or was extremely sexually deprived.

I asked her once, "Angel, do you suppose a certain patient might not have been abused but was spoiled rotten as a child? I remember seeing in stores and school kids who were horrible and out of control, while Mom was spewing out excuses for poor Dick or Jane's behavior."

Angel would come back with, "Of course, I understood that!" I'm not sure how she understood the concept, but her actions said, "I don't think so!" Angel, with her butt swinging, would walk up to a patient and start her snake dance routine—hands on her hip and small chest heaves.

Rules of Confidentiality

Helen, an older lady, was only one of my patients that fateful evening. You could hear her screaming loud, animallike cries and swearing at other patients. She cursed, "Come near me again, you motherfuckers. I've got a black belt in karate! Get your fat ass out of my way!"

Helen grabbed a book, took aim, and threw the book at another patient. The fight was on. All Makai and Mauka were called, and staff responded to the call from the loud overhead speaker system. I, along with four of our psych staff, dove into the first response for wrestling a very obese woman to the floor, getting punched and kicked. Later, two of my staff wound up in the emergency room, and Helen was placed in restraints in her Makai room. This was one of many nights in the psych unit. I was very sore with another set of pulled muscles.

Now I could hear Helen crying. I went to her. For many bipolar patients, the mood swings can change in a split second. One minute Helen could be fighting out of control to wailing, crying for help to a nurse, who's trying to calm her down while the medicine took effect. Helen talked a lot about her nephew, Steve. After supper, I was called to the patients' phone. Helen's nephew, Steve, was on the line. He wanted to talk with his aunt tonight, but she was in restraints in bed.

He waited while I went down and told Helen that Steve was on the phone and wanted to talk with her. Helen said she just couldn't deal with Steve or his dying at death's door from AIDS. Helen asked me to talk with him to see if he could call her later. I told her I would.

I went back and told him, "Your aunt can't come to the phone right now, but she would like me to talk with you and let her know how you're doing."

His voice was weak, yet I could hear him laugh. "I remember you. You were my nurse, bitch! You and all the other fucking bitches! Did I get you? I'm happy. I know a lot of you sanctimonious motherfuckers will be going to my grave with me."

My god, yes. Now I knew who Helen's nephew was. My voice was shaky as I said, "Steve is this you?" Steve was dying of AIDS on another medical floor in the hospital. This was the man I accused of trying to kill me and many others.

"Yeah, bitch. This is none other. I must have infected hundreds. You all thought you were so smart. You and your stupid behavioral contracts. Would you like to hear how many people I was able to infect outside? Did I get you?"

As steady as I could, I tried to find out exactly who Steve had infected with the AIDS virus. However, he was so weak, he faded. Steve died that night. But like thunder in the heavens, my memory was split wide open. Yes, Steve. I remember all your evil and your eyes. It was chilling, like looking into a freezer of bottomless black doom. I remember the never-ending written contracts with Steve to try getting him to stop infecting other patients on our unit with his HIV virus. Steve just kept breaking the contract. We were not prepared for the Steves of the world. It's so clear now. We lived in a world of reality that sometimes goes way beyond recognition of good and evil or right and wrong.

Years ago, I had been Steve's nurse while he was in our acute care psychiatric unit. Steve basically was a depressed sociopath personality, although he also had a psychotic diagnosis, along with a diagnosis of being AIDS positive. Steve spent most of his hospital stay deliberately trying to infect staff and any patient he could seduce or pull his fake "accidental scratch" with contaminated fingernails.

Now as I was remembering Steve's multiple hospitalizations from 1986 to the end of his life, there was utter ignorance of safety and lack of laws for us amid our patients. There were no laws to protect the public. We knew what we needed to do, but we couldn't because of Steve's rights by law and, again, total lack of laws. Steve had, from day one, relentlessly tried to infect anybody he could. It was only after he had been caught having sexual intercourse with one of our female patients that my mentor, Karyl, could take on Steve and the hospital's legal system to try to stop him.

Karyl collected pages of documentation about Steve. Karyl fought hard, but in the end, Steve won. Steve's actions were repeated with the public outside of the hospital. The unit and the general public, our other patients, and staff lost. Steve won after the judge basically didn't know what to do with a patient who was trying to deliberately kill other patients by infecting them. There just weren't any laws for protecting people from the Steves of our world. Thus, Steve was returned to a psych unit with nineteen other patients just to keep doing what he had been doing, trying to kill whoever came near him.

Our nursing supervisor, Flo, was told we could not even tell the other patients about Steve trying to infect patients with his AIDS illness. We were bound to the patient's rules of confidentiality. Flo was told to tell the staff we could not discuss this case with anyone. Flo and Karyl fought to notify the public health department, but that notification was tied up in our upper-level department politics and to my knowledge was never done. The paper trail of Steve was effectively killed at our unit level. Oh, yes, Steve, I remember you well!

Even back then, without the "nail it down to a gnat's ass" documentation and extensive prerequisite paper trails, we grasped the significance of our extreme danger. What we learned through my working years was held and refined: observe, document, bury problems, and keep your mouth shut. We had contacted all the powers that be that we could think of to try to help us. Lu was our hospital's own infection control expert. We called Lu up to the psych unit and asked her to advise us on how to prevent Steve from infecting us and the other patients. Lu really was helpful to Steve, but not to us.

ONE WHO FLEW INTO THE CUCKOO'S NEST

Lu would sit down with Steve and educate him on his disease and how the AIDS virus was spread. I also remember several other people had educated Steve on how the AIDS virus was spread by means other than sexual. Trying to get blood-to-blood contact, Steve would scratch his leg wound and then strike out with his fingernails and scratch other people. He also would spit into other patients' drinks or take bites of their food with liberal saliva.

Lu made sure she documented how well she had armed Steve with her knowledge and education. Her only reference to anybody's safety was by reminding Steve of the staff's written contract with him to not keep trying to infect others. Lu told Steve that we would be watching him for infractions of the contract, without any consequences. For the staff, she told us to keep an eye on him trying to infect other patients and remind him of his contract not to. We explained once again to Lu that we were already watching Steve trying to infect others. We needed to isolate Steve from the other patients. Nope, for Lu there was no need for isolation or increased infection control involvement. However, if we needed her expertise again, we shouldn't hesitate to call her. I can't say I found that action helpful!

We did call her a couple of months later with another one of Steve's admissions. Steve was pulling his continued determination to kill anybody he could get his hands on by means of spit or sexual focus. Lu once again educated Steve on how to spread his AIDS virus and told us to keep an eye on him. Gee, Lu, how can we ever not thank you for all your lack of help and expertise? Now word spread quickly to the unit about his death. I heard the words, and a shout of glee went through me. He's gone. He's really dead. He can't try to kill another person. Wow, this was big!

Many times, I have wondered how many people wound up with AIDS years later, confused and completely without a clue as to where or how they had gotten infected. Also, how would they try to explain their AIDS infection to a loved one? Later that evening, when I was talking to Helen, she told me that for the last nine years, Steve bragged to her about how many people he had infected. He shared how freely he had infected many of health care workers to casual acquaintances or strangers on the streets of Waikiki or anywhere. To my knowledge, he infected these people without one of the victims ever being warned about Steve's intentions. Steve was well-known to the police. They would pick him up and bring him to our unit. There were no laws against what he was doing. The police tried to get Steve off the streets.

For poor Helen, Steve's aunt, she only made it for about another four months before she committed suicide. Her life was so sad and tormented.

Few Times of Winning and Losing

Then Bing came into the unit. Bing was a whole different end-stage AIDS patient. His kidneys were failing now. He wouldn't live much longer. Bing was scared. His family had abandoned him. Most of his tears were a call for human touch. We did a lot. Many of us would work our activities so we could take turns holding him for a little bit. A few days later, we all knew he was very close to death. Bing was on Kekela and needed to get out of a violent psych unit and down to our medical unit for death and dying patients. Bing had used up all his hospital psych days that Medicare and Medicaid would allow, and we were unable to transfer him directly to another unit.

We had word for the Medicare and Medicaid policy and procedure people—bean counters. We had to discharge him. Bing could barely stand up and wasn't suicidal anymore. Therefore, he could be out of the hospital. Yet Bing didn't have any place to go, and he was dying. We were so upset. His doctor was livid, because he hadn't been given any choice except to write Bing's discharge order. Among ourselves, we had set it up so Bing would get back into the medical unit.

We had called the AIDS support people to meet Bing down outside the ER and get him readmitted in a new dying medical patient unit. So we made the arrangements with AIDS support people that we would bring Bing down to the driveway coming into the ER and discharge him. The AIDS support people would meet us there. Then they could take him up to the ER for admission. We took Bing down there, but nobody was there to pick him up. Nobody could stay with him. We called AIDS, and they said they were running late. So we told Bing to stay put, the AIDS people were on their way. Unknown to us, Bing, who was somewhat disoriented, didn't stay put. He never wandered around on our unit. He was always too weak!

The next day, we called for his new room number, so we could go over and see him. No Bing. Then we called the AIDS personnel asking if they had picked up Bing. They said they got there and saw no Bing. They looked around and left. We went into full panic! Three staff went out to try to find him. They found him lying in the bushes. By now Bing looked really bad. So the staff took him straight into the emergency room, and the ER got him over to the medical unit. We held a toast on the unit. To Hell with Medicare, to Hell with Medicaid, to Hell with insurance deciding who gets and who doesn't get. Bing, you would have died on the streets or possibly in an alley all alone! Bing, you got it! Yeah, yeah, team!

One of our new patients, Cliff, was very entertaining and physically strong at fighting but was most memorable for his use of the words, "Get ready to rumble." Being born in the '40s and raised in the '50s, I knew those words. Some of the staff also knew this phrase and the rest of the staff just looked blank. After we got everything calmed down, we gave the blank-face staff a history lesson on the word *rumble*.

Cliff, at the start of shift, was brought in because he was starting to hear voices (hallucinating) and was frightened. Cliff had been using drugs pretty heavily lately. I'm not sure what his drug of choice was. After he got in the unit and the door locked shut behind him, Cliff decided he was going to leave, and it had to be right now. His only problem was he had threatened to kill some people, and we couldn't release him. Well, Cliff decided staff and locked doors weren't going to contain him and said so, "Okay, get all your motherfuckin' staff here. Get ready for a rumble." Cliff took out three staff, before a total of eight staff could come for a full emergency response. That's why I was passing out patients' cigarettes. Most of the staff were trying to patch each other up, and two were down in the emergency room. Cliff had, with a one-arm swipe, threw me into the wall, so I didn't get the full punches. I was just sore. I also was reflecting on the word *rumble*. I hadn't heard this word since the '50s. It was kind of fun; hadn't heard those words for years.

My eyes wandered over to Matthew, psych assistant (PA). He was still standing upright. I was amazed. After Cliff, our rumble boy, had thrown the unit into turmoil.

Pat, another one of our personality disorders with a brief psychotic episode, decided staff had abused poor Cliff. Pat was verbally hammering at what staff were left about how we should do our jobs. Also, Pat was inciting the other patients to revolt against the staff. At that moment, one of our paranoid schizophrenic patients decided Pat was irritating him. So he rushed at Pat and hit him. Well, Pat reacted. Another round for staff.

At one point in the takedown, Pat had somehow managed to get his hand into Matthew's hair and was bashing Matthew's head into the wall. I got a glimpse of Matthew's face as his head was being propelled into another bounce off the wall. It looked like he couldn't breathe. His eyes looked like they were rolled up into his eyelids. Then when we were fully down, I was right alongside Matthew on the floor and over Pat's lower backside. Pat was a nasty takedown. The worst that happened to me as we were all going down for another round of playing bouncing basketball with the floor was my face wound up in Pat's buttock as he was releasing gas. As I started to push myself up, Pat was screaming that somebody was hurting his "balls." Suddenly, I realized my hand was pushing Pat's balls. In a split second, I lifted my right shoulder, got my hand out, and laid back down with my forearm over Pat's buttocks!

We got Pat restrained. Matthew said he was okay, but we sent him down to ER for a checkup. Then along comes Angel, his nurse. She had been standing in the doorway watching the entire action taking place. Pat was to be her patient. For some reason, she felt strongly that she had everything under control with Pat and that Matthew PA and the rest of us had interfered, causing the problem with Pat. Anyway, she started in with some crazy Monday-morning quarterbacking, right then, right there. She started accusing Matthew of grabbing Pat's testicles and physically abusing a patient. I stepped in and told Angel to back off and let her know I was the one pushing on Pat's testicles.

"Matthew was trying to breathe, Angel! He needed to get his eyes rolled back down, his eyes even with his eye sockets. He can't even hear you! Get away!" This was one episode where Angel and I lost any semblance of courteous communication.

The eventual outcome for Pat's accusation, supported only by Angel, wrote Matthew up for assaulting a patient. When I heard what Angel had done, I couldn't believe it! I immediately went to Flo and told her I was the one hurting Pat's testicles. The only person I saw get really hurt was Matthew. Flo explained there was nothing she could do to stop Angel's right to file a complaint. Angel just continued to maintain her single mindlessness and focus on missing the point. Again, I told Angel I was the one in the place where Pat claimed he was getting hurt. Didn't matter; Matthew was reprimanded and had to go to anger management course.

On the side, I asked Angel, "How is it you always manage not to be around until a violent patient is contained?" In the darkest part of my heart, I wished just once, Angel wouldn't be able to outrun a full-on punch to the jaw.

I was out on the patio for a short break with the smokers when the unit suddenly picked up fast. My head was snapped back to reality.

"Oh, oh." A patient jumped up and hit another patient, Sally, in the back. A catfight was on. A male staff and I ran toward Cindy as she was throwing a chair at us. We grabbed her, fighting and kicking. My leg got kicked hard, and I almost lost my balance. As we were getting her through the patio door, she suddenly pulled her legs up and, with her full weight, let go. The male PA yelped that his rotator cuff was hurt. It messed up his rotator cuff for life. We got her dragged back to her room. Medication was given, and she calmed down. She was safe!

Meanwhile, Sally went into a fully heated pursuit. One PA blocked Sally, while my PA and I were wrestling with Cindy on the bed. While Cindy was screaming, Sally was yelling at her. Finally, the three of us were able to contain the situation. All the other staff were tied up. It was a hot unit tonight.

ER called up to the unit. They had a drunken psychotic patient who was going to need detoxification, and they wanted to get him out of ER and up to the unit now! I told them the unit was too hot, and the staff were still recovering.

Jeez! That made Sam, the ER nurse, mad. "Why are you guys such a bunch of prima donnas? No other unit has to hold off taking a patient. I'm giving you ten minutes and sending him up. He just tore apart two ER psych holding rooms and hurt one of the security guys. We can't keep him down here. We're having emergencies."

I quickly asked the PA if he wanted to go down to ER to check his rotator cuff. He said no. He needed to stay. He was working on Makai and sent over to help us. Suddenly, way less than ten minutes, in came one explosive psychotic and drunk patient with two security guards. As the doors locked behind them, the patient got up out of the wheelchair and started taking us all on. I held on to the two security guards that brought him up and what staff we had left. The security guards said they had to go back down to the ER. I took one strong look at them and stated, "I'm the charge nurse here, and you're staying!"

The patient wound up in bed, medicated and restrained. ER was pissed off with us because we kept their security guards. So what! At that moment, we had way too many problems of our own. I told the ER charge, "Tough luck! You don't have a clue about our emergencies up here!" and slammed the phone down!

Smoke the Peace Pipe

There were some of our patients with mental problems that weren't psychotic. Their problems went under a different diagnostic diagnosis. The patients with the label of personality disorders were neurotic, basically malformed personalities. These patients are usually placed outside of a high acuity psych unit. These people can normally function and need a lot of trained psychiatric verbal therapy, which is totally opposite of our acute unit's job.

Usually, these disorders were not considered treatable in an acute hospital setting by insurance companies. There's one well-known exception I know of, which is suicidal. A suicidal depression, whether or not psychotic depression, needed a psychiatric unit where they could be watched and cared for. This type of patient was extremely difficult to treat, especially when the staff expectation was to treat a true psychosis. I remember in a meeting with one psychiatrist, we had asked him what we were supposed to do with his patient, Mr. X. The psychiatrist couldn't understand our difficulty. Occasionally, these patients had strong tendencies to violence. They were just angry, abnormally violent sane people. Something like a violent abusive husband or wife.

Mr. X was admitted to Makai, the open unit. While on the open unit, he slipped out and went to another part of the hospital and traded punches with a patient over there. He had gone there to collect money or drugs. Both patients were substance abusers. We called the doctor and told him that Mr. X was acting more like a criminal than a patient.

"Well," the doctor said, "the patient was depressed and also a substance abuser." Next thing we knew, Mr. X had taken off and came back hours later full of alcohol and cocaine. We called the doctor again. We wanted this patient out of the unit. We did not believe this man was dangerous, at least not in the psychiatric sense. He was somebody who needed to be locked up in jail.

Well, the doctor not only disagreed but also told us his patient needed to be put in the locked unit, Mauka. By the next day, curiously, Mr. X started having a lot of visitors. Staff walked in on a five-hundred-dollar drug deal in progress. Bottom line was, Mr. X was doing his drug buying and selling from the unit, and we had a very heated discussion with Mr. X's doctor about getting Mr. X out of the unit and off to jail. Keeping his drug habit alive and well was not something we were prepared to deal with. We had our hands full with really psychotic patients. Eventually, Mr. X was discharged about two weeks later. We heard he was found murdered in his home, and his home had been burnt to the ground. That's when we found out he had been in the unit for protection from the realities of justice in the drug world. I felt sad for another human being, who was completely unable to alter his life and had been murdered. I felt sorry for him.

For years, our staff would have battles over this type of patient. We couldn't agree on how to care for a patient with a personality disorder and substance abuse. Staff were split, just like Mom and Dad were over disciplining a child. Some staff would want to nurture and love the patient: "They just need a lot of TLC (tender, loving care)." Others would want to kick the patient out by the seat of their pants or at least make them obey the rules: "We're not the police and we're tired of being used as three hots and a cot for the substance abusers and dealers."

The best way we could tell a personality disorder versus a psychotic disorder was by medication. Most of our personality disorders were also substance abusers. So usually, a personality disorder patient would chase the staff around the unit, demanding more and more medication. If we didn't give them what they wanted, they would usually keep upping the ante by threatening the staff that they were going to explode. Then somebody would be getting hurt.

To make this even more objectionable for staff, these patients would warn us if they exploded, it would be our fault due to us not providing the care they needed. These are also the patients that sued the most, threatening to kill you when you're getting off work someday. The personality disorder patients were telling the psychotic patients that they were fine and steal their medicine. They would also teach patients how to "cheek" their meds by hiding their meds inside the cheeks of their mouths. The purpose for this was to achieve getting the psychotic patient to "cheek" medication and pass their meds on to another patient. This was a disgusting con job pulled on our totally oblivious psychotic patients.

For psychotic patients, who really needed antipsychotic medications, we would usually have to chase them around the unit trying to get them to take their medicine. Our psychotic patients would be insisting on something like, "I'm fine. The universal council told me the medicine has evil spirits in it, or the television shoots the radar beam into my brain and the electricity goes to the fluids in my body, turning on the green balance. If I take the medicine, my body will be destroyed by the fluids."

Between the medicine chases and staff declaring war on each other's opinions on how to care for a particular patient, we knew if a patient was admitted to the unit with a psychotic problem or personality problem. Finally, with thanks to Karyl and Flo, we figured out what was happening, smoked the peace pipe, and tried to work through the problem. We did it! A patient protocol was developed, and with this protocol, we could reasonably care for patients with personality disorders.

Mark was mentally retarded (MR) and had been doing well in an MR program. Suddenly, his behavior changed. By the time he got to our unit, he was a mess. The first night, he was all over the unit shredding paper. He couldn't stop grabbing everything and tearing it into little pieces. We almost had a riot with the other patients that night. He had destroyed three Bibles, multiple rolls of toilet paper, two telephone books, all the paper towels, every newspaper and magazine, and two fellow patients' diaries. Mark almost got himself killed over shredding the diaries. We finally wrapped his hands with duct tape. Well, that stopped the shredding but created a new obsession. Next thing we saw Mark doing was standing in the bathroom eating his bowel movement like a Baby Ruth. We couldn't keep his taped hands out of his rectum. He was just wild. Many days later, with medication, we finally were able to help him calm down. Eventually, he went back to the MR program.

Worst Nightmare

This starts the story for the fall of my unit. My whole world, with all the years of learning to care for acutely psychotic patients. We had to struggle for over a year with a high-level boss, Bill, who was totally ignorant about acutely psychotic patients. I didn't want to write this part of my story. It's so painful to relive the pure Hell we went through. I can say this to the reader, the rest of the story may seem disjointed at times. There was no way I know how to smoothly put together all the destruction we were experiencing between being engulfed in bureaucratic quicksand and desperately trying to care for our patients Yet this is a problem we have today, people who have control over patients' care without any understanding of how to care for acute psychotic illness. I am trying desperately to understand the egos involved. What makes any person believe they have all the knowledge needed to fit into any job or work that they have never worked in before! All over the country, there are people with lots of education, yet never dealt with an acutely psychotic patient, have a bureaucratic power completely different than the staff that must work with acute psychotic patients' reality.

My patients, when they came to the unit, were in a world of mental pain that I couldn't begin to imagine. They needed to be cared for. Our job was first to get them to rest through medication and hydration as fast as we could. I was facing a boss who came in and told me to get an acutely psychotic patient up because he needed to get out of this bed and go to the unit group session. That would be crazy!

Just think a minute. That would be like making me the boss who's totally ignorant over a medical unit. Imagine me, completely ignorant about caring for medical care, walking into the room of a patient having a heart attack on a medical floor and telling the staff as their boss to get that heart attack patient out of bed and make them do exercises. Hopefully the nurse would tell me flat out to get out! As their boss, I would respond, "I know better than you, get them up and exercise. How much do you want your job?" Another example would be going into the room of a new stroke patient, paralyzed from the waist down, telling the staff that this patient needs to get out of bed and start walking up and down the halls! Hopefully there would be a full staff revolt, and I would get kicked out of there!

Bill was totally ignorant about psychotic patients. Remember when I started in the unit? I was totally ignorant. But at least I agreed I was totally stupid. I also knew I had a whole lot of learning to do. It took me months, at least a year, before I truly felt some confidence in my skills. Nope, Bill knew it all without a clue and absolutely had no need for learning. He was so set in his own mind that he knew everything, he couldn't hear us telling him that he was ignorant. That created so much turmoil for our unit.

What our unit experienced will show our country that when it comes to making laws for acute psychotic patients, our lawmakers have made some bad laws for our patients' care, like the restraints usage! They listened to people who had never had to care for patients in a high acuity psychiatric unit with wild psychotic patients. They listened to people who just knew general emotional patients without high acuity psychotic mental issues.

Anyway, this part of the story was very hard for me to relive, let alone write. I can only ask my readers to hang, please hang with me. I'm giving this last part my best tries. I promise, my readers, if you can hang with me, we might have a happier ending. That potential possibility of a happier ending, I will always hold like a wonderful gift close to my heart. We still need restraints, but maybe in the next round.

The first time I ever saw Bill in the unit, I didn't have a clue as to who he was: staff or patient. He stood at the nursing station and verbally announced he was our new boss. His first order was that we could no longer have any forced medication for patients who wouldn't voluntarily take offered medication. I took one look at Bill, and my first thought was *Who had hired this ignoramus to be over our unit?*

Following his announcement, line staff could no longer have our policy and procedure of three physicians assessing an involuntary patient: a patient forced into the hospital for behavior potentially dangerous to themselves or others. A patient's wishes for medications didn't matter. For patients who were obviously psychotic and beyond any ability to know what their state of mind was, staff knew we had to first medicate them, followed later by staff verbal interventions.

In five minutes, line staff had a complete change of policy without any input, any patient care alternatives, or any idea of how many of us had gotten the same message. Oh, for those of us who got the message, all right? This man was going to be our worst nightmare.

Bureaucratic Destruction and Death

―――∞―――

Juan was admitted that fateful spring day. He was brought into the ER by the police. Here was where Bill, our big boss, came in and started spewing his insane bureaucratic quicksand! Bill insisted we could not force any medications on Juan! Juan was threatening to kill his wife and children. Juan was full of crystal meth, terrified and paranoid. Juan crouched on the floor, mumbling, unable to move, totally immobilized by his thoughts and fears. He spent a few days in this condition.

We knew Juan was in a quagmire of his own hell. We spent a lot of time just trying to get Juan to eat or drink. Liquids just dribbled out of both sides of his lips, along with a swallow reflex, sometimes a choking reflex. He would swallow solid food placed back in his throat. For hours we took turns sitting on the floor with Juan, trying to help him feel safe and offering him medicine to help calm him down. Juan just wanted his wife, refusing any help from us. Juan finally agreed to take medication when his wife came during visiting hours. We knew Juan was going to explode. But there wasn't anything we could do now to prevent his explosion. Bill had tied our hands, without giving us any alternatives to deal with a psychotic patient on the fast track toward exploding. Visiting hours came and went. Juan continued to refuse all medications, even from his wife.

I was standing on the locked unit's patio with patients, when I heard a loud crash. I saw staff running toward the room right around the nursing station. I heard the staff shouting. Juan, in a split second, smashed out a room window with a chair. Juan had managed to smash a heavily protected glass, an extraordinary act of human strength. Staff were jumping out the exposed window, giving chase to Juan. Juan's superhuman physical status, probably the result of a crystal meth adrenaline rush, enabled him to race off. We immediately initiated the warning phone calls to the police, psychiatrist, Flo, and Juan's family.

Flo was very concerned. She was a hands-on kind of former nursing supervisor and knew the patients. At that moment, I wasn't sure if she was our boss or not, but I'd follow her anywhere. Her directive was to make sure we notified the family. I called the home family number, and a young male voice answered the phone. He told me his mother was gone. I asked Juan's son to ask his mother to call our unit right away as something happened to his father. The boy was so polite and friendly. So I talked to him for a few minutes to get a quick assessment. I asked him how old he was. He said, "I'm ten." Next, I asked him if he was in school. What a response I got. He said he loved school. Then he went on to talk about what his plans were for his future. His voice was excited. He talked for some time. I told him, "You are a very impressive young man," and thanked him for sharing his future plans!

Several days later, Flo let us know Juan was dead. Flo, per the report that she was given, stated the Juan had made his way home days later. He had strangled his wife and his oldest daughter. Then he shot the rest of his children and finalized his crazed nightmare by shooting himself.

All I could think of was *Oh my god! They're all dead*. What a tragedy! I couldn't think. Flo didn't say anything else. But I could hear the disgust in her voice. Flo had lost her supervisory position.

I felt so weak, but I still had patients that needed care, so I went back to work. The staff was in shock and more than a few of us were crying. We had been, by word of mouth, told those windows couldn't be broken! We were told they are shatterproof! Now we were justified in our sense of danger, not just because of staff or other patients getting hurt but because we had proof a family was killed. We told our psych director we needed help, not somebody with the arrogant ignorance of a fool micromanaging our unit. She agreed. So what was the outcome? Bill was praised for his good work on helping the unit with state legal medicine compliance. I heard that Juan's psychiatrist quit taking care of patients in the hospital. Flo was, without any cause, not so secretly blamed for what happened to Juan and his family.

When I heard and processed what happened, all I could picture was that little boy, who had to watch as his father strangled his mother and sister! I prayed to God, "Please tell me he hid under a bed, that he didn't have to watch. The terror he must have felt." In that moment, inside my body, I felt a strange, full-boiling angry rage, like I have never felt before or since! My soul inside me was erupting. I had no control, and physically, I felt intense nausea. It was as if my body turned itself into a volcano, and it was going to blow! The next time I saw Bill, my mouth just opened and spewed hot verbal lava all over, lambasting Bill up one side and down the other. I don't remember all the words I said to him, except I remember the exact words at the end, "Condescending bastard!" Finishing off with, "Take your policy about medication and shove it straight up where the sun doesn't shine. From this day forward, I will be giving meds the same way I have for my last many years."

Bill just stared at me, the look in his eyes dove into my eyes, filling me with raw terror, then he turned and walked out of the unit. Suddenly, full of fear, my mind flashed back to my childhood memory with my brother. I was about six. Bill's response called forth a memory of warning from long ago. At our Junction City, Kansas, riverbank, two young children, my brother and I, were standing with our feet barely in the river.

I wanted to play further into the river, but my brother held me back and warned me, "Kid, don't go any deeper in the water. The water only looks safe. Underneath the water is the riverbed. The riverbed isn't what it looks like. It might not just be sand. The bed might have quicksand in it. You never ever know where the quicksand is until it's too late. The quicksand sucks you in and swallows you! You will suffocate. You will be dead!"

Now my brother lives far away from me. I jumped straight into the unit's bureaucratic quicksand. I'm going down! I didn't know what to do! I couldn't save myself or my patients! What on God's green earth is going to happen to our patients? To this day, I don't know where Juan's son was. God never told me. And now that young boy would be in his late thirties. But now he's just dead and all his excitement about his future dreams were killed! I have to and do live everyday with the loss of that young man's possible needless death.

This part of the story, at the end of my wonderful years with Barb and Flo as our bosses, had a very quick and dramatic sudden ending.

Bureaucratic Quicksand

〜

This process for staff was like falling into a pit of suffocating bureaucratic quicksand! Suddenly, changes started falling out of the sky. Staff didn't have a clue about what we were supposed to be doing. Suddenly, Bill appeared in the unit and told us he was officially the new administrator for our unit! He was never, as far as we knew, in any way part of any psychotic unit before, but we heard he was very close friends with Duane, who was newly appointed to the position of vice president over all the hospital's nurses. Duane came out of the surgery unit. My friends who worked in surgery didn't have one nice word to say about him.

Bill was only about giving mandates, without getting staff together to hear what the changes were. Nor was there any reality about new written policies that we knew of, just verbal promises of new policies coming. The upshot of this was the announcements here and there had very little, if anything, formalization. We didn't know what to do. So most of the older staff, like me, just kept doing what we had always done. Flo wasn't there, but her spirit was.

A picture of what was and what was to come floated through my head. I could see what was on their minds, total ignorance. Suddenly, it was crystal clear that our patients, at this rate, would lose the care they needed. These managers lived in a moronic world of nonreality by claiming our patients were rational and had rights! My patients were almost always totally out of contact with anything that looked close to rationality. Immediately, I felt like I was being asked to take what amounted to an old, abandoned bus, cast off to the side in a junkyard, and we were being told by idiots to get the bus moving down the road. No wheels, no motor—just go! I kept getting stuck with the idea as to how we were supposed to make this bus move. We'd asked for a mechanic, and they sent us a tour guide. The real plan seemed to be to harness us up to the bus, with tasseled Clydesdales, and manually pull the bus to show us off to who knows where. Then we could bring out our new magic wands and claim our patients were well.

I was beginning to get a hint of the real plan. All this had something to do with money and models of psych units in other parts of the country. Insurance companies pay a set rate for hospital rooms but must pay extra for any provable extra therapy, like group therapy. This was about money and somebody's ego. For us workers, the real culprit would probably never be known to us. The destruction of quality patient care would be devastating to our psychotic patients! Honestly, I can say since our hospital took on all the "give us your tired and poor," we rarely got the well-endowed paying customers.

I was not sure why, but one day, Flo, before she left, asked me to join her in a "they" kind of meeting. Maybe Flo, as her days on the unit were numbered, decided she'd get a kick out of my reaction to one of those meetings? Sitting in a meeting with Flo, Sara, Bill, and two support services, the unveiling took place of the unit plan program. The plan was many pages long and was about to be launched onto the highest acute psychiatric patients, which never worked down to the floor staff. I looked at it like I might watch a cockroach walk across a plate of food. Sara was standing and describing all the new and wonderful plans for our patients. One of the first plans was to get every patient up at 0630 dressed in street clothes: "Patients will no longer have hospital clothes. All hospital clothing is going to be removed from the unit. All the patients will be up dressed and in the day room." Then the patients would attend a day filled with different groups, which Sara, Thumper as I had nicknamed my immediate idiot supervisor, and Bill had in their infinite ignorance designed. I asked, "Do you mean all the patients?"

"Yes, Ginger, I mean each and every patient! We will not tolerate any negativity about this!"

I had the feeling Sara was on the defensive with me, but I just couldn't resist. "Sara, are you telling me that, after we spent half a shift trying to knock a patient out, you want us, in less than eight hours, to try and get this medicated patient up out of bed so we can chase him around the unit for another whole shift trying to knock him out again?"

Bill's face turned purple, and words just sputtered out, "Ginger, what you mean by knocking a patient out?"

Flo intervened here. "What Ginger means is medicating a violent patient."

Bill, leery now, said, "Oh, I thought Ginger was saying they took baseball bats to the patients or something."

After that, I just listened, my mind returning to last night on the unit. We had three critical patients. One patient came in loaded with crystal meth. He'd been sleep deprived for days. His urine looked like close to rusty water. I was afraid his liver and kidneys might fail. His blood pressure was going off the Richter scale. I called his psychiatrist and told him about the urine concern. He said he would order IV to come up and hang a bag of fluids on him. He had the bag for about twelve hours. I was told by the next day his urine was cleared.

His skin was one solid crust of wounds, after running through bushes with thorns. His thoughts were "Everyone is going to kill me, so I needed to kill them first." We had managed to get a full two cups of water into him before the shot of Haldol put him to sleep. Bill wanted us to get this person up, dressed, and ready for "the program"? I don't think so. I asked about it the next day, and the nurse said, "No way. He slept most of the day!" When he woke up, we took him down to the shower and got him cleaned up, and that was a big project. Then we got some food and oral fluids into him. He was ramping up by then, and he took a pill and went back to sleep.

The other patient was Ella, who was well-known to us. She was a seventy-seven-year-old woman about three hundred pounds. Ella also had stress incontinence. For the first stage of any of her admissions, she was not safe. Ella had this tendency to urinate and defecate everywhere. Also, when she got mad, which was at least once every half-hour, she'd grab other patients or staff with her hands full of feces and scratch them. The other patients in return would slap and say many unkind words to Ella. Ella usually needed a very quiet room for a few days and lots of cleaning up before she was ready for any social intervention. What she needed was time and medication. Not to mention, Ella had only come in with one set of clothes. We supplied another set of clothes, which she needed. Staff kept loading up the washer and dryer multiple times a day when Ella was in the unit.

The Big Plan

Speaking about clothes and the unit realizing most patients just came in with just the clothes on their back, many times their clothes were in rags. We had to have clothes in the unit on hand for these patients. Some of the staff would buy clothes at Goodwill and clothing was donated to the hospital. It was always a struggle to get clothes for patients.

Once, I remember a well-endowed...bosom elderly lady who came into the unit, with a bullet hole in her breast. A policeman had accidently shot her breast through a door. My partner and I went out and bought her a bra. Scrubs were not available to our patients. However, we could use scrubs for covering when we were desperate, which was fairly often. We washed a lot of clothes.

The last patient was Trudy. Trudy was bulimic and her potassium level was 2.1. This meant Trudy was a hair's breadth away from death at any given moment. We couldn't let anybody near her because Trudy would con the other patients into getting her water so she could puke some more. One more round of vomiting could possibly mean death. The previous night, Trudy had gotten out of her room and attempted to yank out her TPN line (IV line that goes straight to into a vein) and tried to drink it. I, along with another staff, wound up rolling on the floor in a full fight trying to keep the line in. Fluids were flying everywhere. Oh, yeah, I can just see it. Trudy, with every group, making mad dashes for the water fountain, sink, shower, toilet, anything with fluid, or Trudy trying to pull her line out again and potentially bleeding to death in the middle of the group. After we got her settled down, we got an IV team to come and get her hooked back up. The other patients were always clamoring for us to be kinder to poor Trudy and let her have just one little drink. Due to confidentiality, we couldn't announce to the other patients Trudy's condition.

Okay, I had to snap my mind back to the meeting as it was so boring. I looked up at Sara and Bill, asking who would be running all these groups. Sara informed me that the nurses would.

I asked Bill, "When would this program be starting?"

Bill casually announced, "Next week."

I asked Bill, "If the nurses would be starting to run the program next week, what's the plan for teaching the nurses how to run the groups? Also, how are we going to be taking care of the medically compromised patients, plus all the patients' ADL's (activities of daily living) and run the groups all at once? Let alone," I continued, "how did you want us to get the violent patients up and out?"

Then I went on to ask that since this was all going to be taking place next week, "Bill, wouldn't it be a good idea to let the staff know what the plan is, because nobody has told us there was going to be a plan?"

Sara's face was priceless. "Ginger, we haven't completed the plan yet. The plan will be done in a few days. Bill will most certainly be helping to implement the plan on the unit!" Well, Bill never showed up to initiate any plan!

I responded, "But, Sara, Bill doesn't do that very well. Remember Juan and his family?"

Flo, by now, was softly kicking my foot under the table. Thumper and Bill looked like they might want to permanently shut my mouth soon. So Flo asked me if it was time to leave. I looked at Flo. Yes, it's time to leave. Flo never said a word after we left. But in her eyes, as we looked at each other, I saw what she had been battling and why she couldn't have made it bureaucratically.

Shortly thereafter, Flo, in her final staff meeting with us, told us officially that she was offered a new position and would be resigning as our head nurse. However, she would still be in and out of the unit with a different job and title.

Now wait a minute. Flo had started in this unit many years ago. She had built herself up from a PA to our nursing supervisor. "What's really going on, Flo?"

Flo stared ahead for a while and looked to us like she was trying to choose her words carefully. "I'm not able to speak freely. That is for upper management to do. I will say this. Accept what changes are coming. I'm not like the captain of a ship. I'm not going to sink with the ship."

My heart sank. How much were we in for? Flo's last words drove home the scope of what was to come. Flo continued, "Bill has asked Sara to act as your supervisor, until the process for finding my replacement is completed."

I couldn't believe my ears. Sara? The two-year degreed nurse on the unit who was terrified of anything remotely connected to a fighting patient and ran from any struggling psychotic patient while calling for staff. However, she was good with patients swapping drug stories, story for story, with our substance abusers. What in God's name are Bill and our Vice President Duane thinking of? I left the meeting and went straight to Sara and asked, "What in the Sam Hill is going on?"

Sara gave me that Cheshire cat smile and informed me, "Ginger, you know I was a cheerleader. Also, Bill didn't want me to say anything. But since you're my friend (only in her mind), I'll tell you. The unit is in for big changes. Bill has been after me for weeks to replace Flo. Flo is just too controlling, and we need to be very flexible now."

I asked, "What kind of big changes? Sara, are we talking about changes like people not getting assaulted anymore or like we might have a couple of days' notice before somebody decides to change a policy or, gee, something special like somebody sitting down with all our new staff and educating them about dealing with mentally ill patients?"

Sara's response was "Now, Ginger, don't start out negative. We have big plans to make this unit profitable, and we don't want any negativity!" And so the big plan had nothing to do with our patients; this was simply about money! The plan was so divorced from the reality of our patients' needs. Our patients couldn't come close to performing, which Bill and Sara were expecting of them!

So life went on in the unit as usual. Lynda from risk management knew very little about our unit and indicated a reluctance to learn about the way our unit had to function. I had met her in our unit during an investigation into the death of a patient, Mr. Y. Mr. Y's death taught me the lesson of how Lynda dictated the view of death in our unit. Mr. Y had been in and out of the unit for years. During his last admission, Mr. Y had followed his natural pattern. He had become violent and started a fight. Staff restrained him and got him calmed down. Mr. Y, medicated and fresh out of restraints, went into an almost catatonic female patient's room and attempted to relieve his sexual needs. According to Mr. Y, he was one of the best of the best male stud horses, which any female would want. We were supposed to be sorry for him and understanding. Well, we weren't, and Mr. Y got violent again.

The next day, we finally were able to get him calmed down. Around 3:00 p.m., Mr. Y started escalating and getting angry, demanding a bath. "Now!" He wasn't my patient, but I thought a warm bath might settle him down. I asked his nurse Karyl. She agreed. So I took Mr. Y to the tub room. Just before the change of shift at 3:30 p.m., Karyl knocked on the door and asked him how he was doing at about 3:25 p.m. Mr. Y's response was "I'm fine. How are you doing?" Well, those were the last words he ever spoke.

By the time I got home, the coroner's office was calling me, wanting to know what I had done to Mr. Y. I told them, "Gave him a bath." Well, Mr. Y, shortly after we left, was found dead in the bathtub. I told them Mr. Y was in his early seventies and that wouldn't be unusual, considering he had a long drinking history and had been acutely physically stressed lately.

That was my first meeting with Lynda and risk management. Some family finally crawled out of the woodwork, even though they hadn't had anything to do with Mr. Y for years. They had probably been afraid of him. I would guess the family needed to protect their children from Mr. Y, probably afraid of what he might do to their children sexually. I would agree with the family; he could possibly be very dangerous to their children. Now they were mourning the loss of a family member.

Lynda let me know I was under investigation for negligent homicide. Also, Lynda let me know that there weren't supposed to be any deaths on a psych unit. If water was found in Mr. Y's lungs indicating he had drowned, I would probably be charged with homicide. I was shocked! Letting a man have a bath? Now wait a minute! Mr. Y had a great last day. He'd had his favorite things. We learned later he had sex with a willing female patient, slapped two staff, including myself, and ate a very nice meal. The only reason he was in the tub was hopefully to prevent another round of restraints. I told Lynda to think of it like a service. "Mr. Y had been living on the streets. Yet for his finale, he had all his needs meet."

"Ginger, are you saying there was sex in the unit?"

"Yes, Lynda. It isn't that unusual. Haven't you been reviewing the incident reports we have been generating and asking for help?" Some highly acute insane patients have very intense sex drives.

Coroner reports take a long time. Waiting was horrible. Finally, the report came back. No water in the lungs. He had apparently had a heart attack. However, to fix the problem of patients dying in the unit, we had to lock the tub room and staff had to sit with a patient for any baths. Just as I thought. Nothing short of a brilliant half-thought-out legal move by Lynda, who could have come up with such a solution. So we stopped allowing most patients to have baths. We didn't have enough staff to sit by a tub for a long relaxing bath. Now we can only give baths to our fighting patients, with gross layers of filth and/or insect infestations.

On the head of the list was a middle-aged patient, Diane, who had been brought in manic, out of control, with a foul-smelling greenish vaginal discharge. Her fingernails were full, long unbroken claws. She was clawing at us in full combat mode. Her arms were immediately placed in a waist restraint, along with a shot. Then we clipped her fingernails, which also took several staff, while she was trying to pull away. It took quite a while, but we did it. She still had very short nails. The lady was filthy dirty and needed a bath. One patient slapped her for smelling bad. So quickly, Harriet had a bath, which was quite a project. Three staff received multiple scratch wounds.

Another female patient, a street person, came in with the multiple layers of filth. Her matted hair was full of nesting insects and bathing her was quite a fight. She fought six staff, including a couple staff from Makai, while we bathed her and cleaned her up. With the tub, we could get three staff on each side and holding on to a scratching, kicking, spitting, and slippery female was quite a feat. It took us three full baths to get her hair and scalp cleaned and combed out. We generated the paperwork and sent it through the system. Never heard back from her or anybody's current paperwork. Our report probably landed in Lynda's risk management inconsequential box of who cares.

Back at the unit, Rocky, the big football player at the beginning of my story, by the end of his stay, was always like a big teddy bear. Well, Rocky was back in the unit again. However, this time, Rocky was tragically not the same Rocky. He wound up learning the scariest news anybody can ever get! He had stopped taking his medication because his kidneys were failing after heavy doses of Lithium. I looked at him as I was coming out of the report room. His hostile fixed eyes penetrated me. Every hair on my neck stood at attention. Within an hour, Rocky decided he was going to take us all on. It went fast. Luckily, we had three good-sized men. By the time Rocky was contained, there were at least four female and male staff on the floor. When I got up off the pile of humanity, I sat on the side of the bed and just looked. Legs, arms, elbows, rear ends were everywhere, and Rocky wasn't giving up. It took us about fifteen minutes to anchor Rocky and get all the staff up off the floor. Yet the worst was to come.

Later, Rocky conned one of the staff to release one leg restraint and one wrist restraint for supper. Big mistake. Rocky ate all right.

Then, as the staff was removing his tray, Rocky's gigantic fist punched the PA. All of us came on a full run. I was trying to hold Rocky's shoulder down with another staff. I could feel the steel muscles ripple out from under my full weight, and the PA on the left got that explosive steel fist in his face at least twice. Yet we couldn't really medicate Rocky. Medication might kill him. After that, the doctor tried him on a low level of medications, and we barely were able to get Rocky into a mellow state. Then the bad news came. Rocky's labs indicated the years of medication had severely damaged his liver. He only had approximately two years to live.

By now, Rocky was like a big soft wooly bear. He had a great sense of humor and was so gentle. His mother was the main person in Rocky's life. Together they had to make a very difficult decision. His mother clearly told Rocky what his choices were to keep taking the medication and stay with his mother to the end of his life or quit the medication, which was killing him, and be placed in a long-term state mental hospital. His mother couldn't handle Rocky when he was in a manic state because of his extreme violence.

She knew he would kill her eventually, and each time he got out of control, he destroyed all the furniture in the house along with toasters, refrigerator door, fixtures, you name it. At one time or another, Rocky had destroyed it all. But most of all, she was terrified of him. Rocky decided on taking the medication and wanted to have the rest of his life at home with his mom.

He should have died two years later. Those of us who remember him cried for him. Right now, while writing this, my heart hurts. Here I was, typing like a big baby, crying with tears along with a runny nose running down my face. Rocky, right now, hope you're in heaven playing football. You are surely missed by the very staff you tried to tear apart. You showed us what a great, lovable man you really were. Rocky, by now, your mother must have passed. She was a great woman and loved you with a force that few could match from the beginning to the end of your life! Hats off to Mom.

Nothing but Frustration

We were told we couldn't use restraints. Jim was a new and very violent patient on the unit. We sent the message to the nursing union about Jim. They were very helpful. They sent each of us a brochure from the American Nurses Association on Violence in The Healthcare Workplace. Also, the union promised to help with any meetings we wanted. They also told us to be sure to keep documenting as, "The nursing union needs a paper trail." In all the time to come, the only action which staff could get from their cries for help was either to be told to talk about the problem or to document the problem. Pure garbage!

I talked with Sara to learn if we could get some help with Jim. Too many people were getting hurt, and she was our boss, so she needed to tell us how to handle violent patients. The unit didn't have any choice, so we had to use restraints. We just didn't bother telling our bosses. Sara wrote a big note to the staff about using our "alternatives and professional skills." We were asking for help with a violent patient, without being able to use restraints.

Suddenly, Sara was all over me to get our staff educated about the new restraint policy, although there wasn't any sessions schedule for educating set up for a new policy! Sara told me, "All you folks need is to complete the self-learning modules on restraints. It's imperative that you are clear on these policies…" I told Sara we had two new restraint policies and procedures (P&P). Since they were different, which one was we supposed to follow? Also, both the P&Ps called for a padded room, which our unit doesn't have.

"Sara, you aren't hearing my question. I'm asking you, what alternatives? We had PAs and nurses who had been on the unit less than three weeks trying to train more new staff. More experienced staff were fleeing the sinking ship or being pushed overboard. Tell us how to handle violent patients without restraints. We can't just throw up an abracadabra magical shield around us for protection. Patients and staff were taking physical blows. There was no holding a violent patient back. Sara, after you physically grab them by their arms, then what? Walk them back to their rooms? They just walk back out again!"

Now Sara's response changed to "Ginger, I didn't have anything to do with the walking restraints being discontinued. Bill was told by risk management that walking restraints were illegal."

That sent me straight to Lynda, head of risk management. I asked her how she had decided walking restraints were illegal and what were our alternatives. Lynda said she didn't know anything about it. "Ginger, that is a unit's decision."

So then I went to Bill and asked why he had decided walking restraints had to be discontinued. Bill said, "Lynda told me they were illegal. Ginger, there wasn't anything I could do."

I informed Bill I had just come from Lynda's office and told him that he was lying to me. Bill exploded, "Ginger, I don't like to see walking restraints and we are trying to build compliance with state law."

Yet there hadn't been any state law; it was just talk! I demanded, "Bill, I want to see this state law!" Here's where I got thrown out of his office. Sometime later, a very contrite Bill told us to use restraints.

Without saying a word, and while I was working that evening shift, I told my staff to put Jeff in walking restraints. Our shift never had another problem with Jeff; he did fine. Nobody ever got hurt on our shift. Word got around, and all the other nurses started using the walking restraints. It got a lot calmer on the unit. Sara and Bill weren't really interested in coming into the unit to check on what we did or didn't do with the patients. They never said anything to any of us about walking restraints. Jeff's behavior got under control, and he did really well! We just kept using restraints. We didn't have any alternatives.

Then the reason why came. "This is a Department of Health thing…we need to be in compliance. Also, we have to be ready for Joint Commission on Accreditation of Healthcare Organizations (JCAHO)."

"Oh, I get it. Lying to staff and to the union is fine, but right now, we need to have pieces of paper so we can lie to the Health Department and JCAHO."

Sara wasn't finished with me yet. "Ginger, you're not doing your job. We're only going to be keeping the nurses who get involved with the unit—besides just taking care of patients." Sara was right about that, though I didn't care for the not-so-veiled threat to my job. I never could figure out why I wasn't fired. I sure should have been. I broke more of their new policies than I could count!

Back to the world of unit reality, on Makai we had a very depressed, verbally abusive patient. Without gender, I will name this patient Sawyer. Sawyer was a very bright, smart, and highly educated person. Sawyer had climbed all the way up to a top executive position in a very powerful institution. That takes a lot of smarts and know-how! Sawyer retired. Sawyer didn't have any back-up life for being alone. Sawyer started excessive drinking. Sawyer got very loud and abusive when talking about family. Sawyer's PA noted deep emotional heavy crying, which was especially painful when talking about family. The PA noted Sawyer didn't say anything specific about family. However, the way Sawyer erupted led the PA to think something must have happened at a relatively young age, which had wounded Sawyer for life. Sawyer never stated any events but had a particular negative focus on one family member, without making any direct accusations.

Now without anything else in life to look forward to, Sawyer just lived in the past and drank. Many times, Sawyer came through the unit. Staff found Sawyer the same accusatory and verbally abusive patient. Sawyer rejected all staff, except one PA, who was an older man in his fifties. He would let Sawyer vent and never respond. Finally, Sawyer would wear out and sit down with him and start talking. Sawyer demanded for that PA every time Sawyer came to the unit. The nurses were fine with that. The last time Sawyer came to the unit, Sawyer was as usual very inebriated, swearing and verbally abusive, wanting Sawyer's usual personal PA who was on vacation. When Sawyer left, Sawyer went down to a Honolulu hotel. Got a room on the highest floor and jumped to Sawyer's death. This news went around the unit fast. The PA came back from vacation, but none of the staff wanted to tell him what Sawyer did. Finally, a week later, a nurse told the PA what Sawyer had done. He felt sorry for Sawyer and still thinks sometimes about Sawyer and feels sorry for that person to this day!

Nursing Care Breakthrough, Yeah!

We sometimes had very close calls with patients. An elderly female was in the unit for depression. We were told she had a heart doctor. She wasn't my patient, but one day, her PA asked me to take a listen to her heart. I did and it sounded strange, but I knew her heart doctor was coming in to see her. So I told the PA we will wait until the heart doctor sees her.

He came in shortly after that and saw her. As he was leaving, I asked him how her heart was doing. He disdainfully gave me a glaring look, staring straight at me. "Her heart is just fine," and walked out of the unit. But I couldn't rid myself of feeling something was wrong. As soon as he left the unit, I made, without doctor authorization, a telephone order for her to have an EKG. An EKG tech came up, hooked her up, let out a little yelp, then full steam ahead, staff got her over to the intensive care unit! She was having some sort of heart attack or issues, and luckily, we caught it. I never heard back from the heart doctor, nor did I get reported for the telephone order.

Also, all the new staff hadn't really been in Kekela long enough to know the systems in the hospital and how to access the resources a patient might need. I caught the heart attack by sheer instinct, and it was helpful not to be thinking like a P&P robot nurse. The lady survived, but it was close. This happens rarely, but occasionally it just happens! I just always wanted to stay with the patients and be left alone. I had already been taught not to trust meaningless Policy and Procedure words, while staff were being hung high.

I want to mention here that during all my later years, I took quite a few telephone calls ordered by doctors, and mainly resident students in the last years of finishing their residencies, without calling them. I just adored the residents. I would always kid them and charge them for writing a medication order for them that they forgot. They mostly kept forgetting to write the patient request medication or PRN. I would always tease them, "Okay, I had to cover your ass. The going price is one box of chocolate-covered macadamias nuts." The regular doctors hardly ever forgot, but every once in a while, it happens.

One time, it was Dr. Coleman, the head of the whole psychiatric unit. She forgot a PRN medication, and I told her that I knew how powerful she was but she still had to pay up! Dr. Coleman coldly looked at me and stated, "You mean, you are going to charge me!"

I said, "Yep, I charge everybody else!"

She replied, "How much?" I told her. She just turned and walked out.

The next day, she came in with her box of candy and said, "I expect to get one of these!"

"Yes, ma'am. I always shared the box with all the staff." This was always a fun time eating Ginger's chocolates as they called it.

Sara had spent the greater part of her first year working with her hospital task force to develop a two-sentence mission statement that basically said, "The Queen's Medical Center is committed to leadership and preserving, protecting, and perpetuating the health of all people…We shall accomplish this mission through education, research, and the provision of quality health care…"

Wow, what an extensive piece of work that must have been for Sara. Two paragraphs in one year? Sara was a very busy lady. All these task groups came in between her days away and vacations. She came back from a one day-away encounter group where she had gotten in touch with her psychic inner self. She was upset when she came back and didn't feel the staff were in harmony with each other. So she sent out notes about "The Holy Encounter" and "When you meet anyone, remember, it is a holy encounter. As you see him, you will see yourself…"

Between all the administrative mental health goodies and not-so-subtle threats, I stood still and thought, *How does this all come together with the patient or floor experience?* Maybe I'm supposed to be preaching all this warm and fuzzy stuff to my patients? Well, just maybe, it'll work, and I tried to be warm and fuzzy with a patient, Jim. Jim was one of our major psychotic disorders. His reaction to warm and fuzzy was to pick up a large chair and throw it into the nursing station at me. He took out the phone system and a couple of staff. I haven't given up warm and fuzzy yet. I tried it with Todd.

Todd was a manic patient and having a bad hair day. After failing with Jim, I finished trying to subdue Todd with "Isn't life just like a grand bowl of cherries?"

His chart read, "Assaultive threatening behavior; aggressive toward staff; struck staff; combative, placed in restraints stating, 'I'll kick your asses'; struck another patient, connecting right fist to other patient's left temporal area."

Later, Todd was agitated. We told him to go to his room. Todd shouted, "I'm not going to my room, and you're not big enough to make me. If you try, you're fuckin' dead."

I think Sara lost her grasp of floor reality. I decided administration had broken from reality and lived in the ivory tower where a lot of our schizophrenics stayed. My mentor's words came to me, "Listen to what's being said, but keep your focus on the patients and where they're at." I wanted my paycheck; but I didn't really want to die for it.

Wait a minute. By a patient and while on duty, I've already done that! I got AIDS, trying to remember what year this revelation all took place—I got infected in about 1986 and should have already been dead by 1989. Here in about 1997, I was alive and not sick. My doctor told me my blood work was terrible. Life expectancy for AIDS patients back then was two years. Huh! There was no medicine for AIDS until about 1997!

Infection Control Fantasy

I was going over the P&P book and discovered a brand-new P&P about medications. I simply couldn't believe it. Bill had put in a whole new backdated policy about medications. Bill hadn't even told any of the nurses he just changed our whole medication P&P. The nurses on the floor were giving medications totally illegally! He was adding a lot of policies to the P&P book for our upcoming Joint Commission on Accreditation of Healthcare Organizations (JCAHO). However, Bill never bothered to tell us about the new policies. The policies were just placed in the book.

I went straight to Bill and wanted to know whatever possessed him to back draft a new policy without telling anyone. He had just placed all the nurses in our unit at risk of losing their licenses. His response was "The policy needed to be updated for JCAHO and Sara was supposed to let you all know." Of course, Sara denied this. What was incomprehensible to me was Bill didn't have a clue that he had totally legally compromised every nurse in our unit.

The second thing that started a stir in me was when a patient with hepatitis C kept spitting into a nurse's face during her admission, stating, "I hear it's very infectious. Want some?"

When we called infection control, we wound up fighting to get any help with follow-up. That did it. I was ready to jump headlong into the politically correct delusional world that "Working staff is empowered." Knowingly, I stupidly headed for an exhausting round of getting nowhere! All right, Sara, I'll join one of your task forces. There are only three things that really interest me: legal P&P, violence, and infection control on our unit.

I had also told the nursing union how the focus was shifting away from patient care. The gals there were shocked about the conditions but gave the good old standby: "Keep documenting. We need a paper trail." The union also wondered why the other nurses weren't coming forward with these problems.

I said to them, "Sara has many of the nurses completely intimidated. If one of the staff even suggested there was a problem, the staff's attitude became the problem, and they would be encouraged to quit or be threatened with a trumped-up disciplinary action. That was Sara's solution."

So I lined out in my head what we needed to be educated on: the restraint policy, the medication policy, and the need to take a long look at infection control in the unit. Infection control was agreed upon as being the most important. Infection control has always been an ongoing problem for psychiatric patients and staff. The only response we could ever get out of Lu was "You guys don't have many exposures up here."

First, I started by sitting down with Lu and having a real heart-to-heart talk about our exposures. I naively thought if Lu could understand our patients, she would be able to see our problems. Talk about pounding your head on a brick wall. No number of words could overcome her desire not to know.

I spent about an hour trying to tell her how patients and staff were being exposed to serious infections. I reviewed our patient Tammy, who was a patient with a MRSA infection. MRSA infections are the most virulent and easily transmitted of all staph infections. For any other part of the hospital, Tammy should have been placed in isolation, but here we didn't have isolation rooms. Tammy was out walking around with all the other patients. We had called Lu.

ONE WHO FLEW INTO THE CUCKOO'S NEST

She told us to have Tammy keep her hands clean and the wounds covered. Well, Tammy couldn't go along with the plan.

So Tammy was running around the unit itching her wounds and touching everything from the unit's community water fountain, telephone, food, and people. Normally this would be an immediate transfer to isolation for a normal hospitalized person. Not for us. We couldn't even get a culture check for ourselves to see if any of Tammy's wounds had infected us or other patients who had wounds. Our psychiatrists weren't very happy about this and were quite concerned for their patients. I went over with Lu and her lack of psych infection awareness and how we needed to combine her specialty with our reality. All Lu could say was "Sorry, this is your problem."

With the AIDS epidemic, the whole focus on health care was ER (emergency room), OR (operating room), and staff getting poked by needles. Around 1989, after a nurse at our hospital had been exposed and contracted HIV from a needle poke, the newspapers were reporting all the nonexistent programs that had been set up for our hospital.

"Lu (infection control nurse), do you remember the health department report about how compliant the hospital is with exposures? Yet we can't get you to help or follow-up with our exposures or prevention of exposures. Also, remember the report you said you gave to Duane so he could confirm that all our exposure center's health care workers practice 'body substance isolation' and infection control methods that requires the use of gloves, gowns, masks, or protective eyewear when dealing with blood or body substances?" I asked her.

"Lu, you know what you said isn't true. It does not happen for us! Yet just from needle pokes and splashes as the most common exposure in this state from 1990 to 1991, there were 930 exposures reported. Who is going to lead us for infection with the psychiatric patient population and workers' exposures? Exposures they aren't even aware of. What do we say for them?" I continued.

I know what to do. Just tell them to call infection control and let Lu just lie to exposed patients or workers!

I told Lu I had gone to our employee health physician and reviewed with her the exposures on our unit and how they were being missed. For instance, the unit had an AIDS patient who was deliberately trying to infect others again on the unit. He had sex with a sixteen-year-old patient on the unit. When confronted, his response was "I told her I had the disease, but she still wanted me to bang her." Also, he would masturbate, and he would smear his semen onto another patient. Once again, we couldn't get the hospital systems to respond to protect us. We were just trapped with him. I will add here there were no laws that protected people against trying to peacefully infect another human. The hospital fought for laws. This took a very long time. It took like years for state legislatures to create such laws.

Masturbation was a big problem in our unit. Many manic patients, when in a manic high, are very sexually preoccupied.

"Lu, we just had a patient, who never had her hands out of her leaking crotch, scratch a security person during a nasty takedown. I called down to the ER to find out what was the follow-up plan for exposure. I was told there was none and 'scratches aren't high risk,' I said.

"Lu, you know better than this. Any patient who is constantly masturbating then scratches another human being and rips open the flesh while depositing their sexual fluids has got to be at a high-risk exposure! How could that possibly be different from sexual intercourse? Lu, try to think about this like a patient giving a shot of VD straight into a person's arm, face, back, legs, wherever."

Lu said she was going to a National Convention for Infection Control Nursing and would see what was happening in the nation on psych unit exposures and if they were being treated differently. A couple weeks later, I looked Lu up and asked her what the infection control nurses were doing nationwide as a whole for psych patients and psych staff regarding their unique exposure risk.

Lu said they did not see it as vastly different from what ER had said, "Scratches weren't a very high risk." The focus remained on needle pokes, using gloves, and universal precautions. I knew immediately she had not talked with any nurses who worked with the high acuity patients. There was a big, big difference between unmedicated, totally out of control patients and patients who are medicated and with some potential of reality baseline.

Universal precautions. Lu's responses were always the same, "Ginger, you're just so negative! What are we supposed to do? We could encase you all in plastic…"

My response was "Lu, don't you give a damn about us?"

By then we had another patient in the unit with MRSA infection. I asked Lu if we could get help. She said there was nothing she could do. So I developed a paper trail, thinking maybe the union would help.

Lost Infection Fight

Remembering our honest typical working conditions policy and procedures for work: *Exposure to body fluids, blood products, and communicable diseases.* That was written in 2022. At least it's honest.

I will mention here that the morning groups on Mauka had become hit or miss. Then I rarely heard any more about them. I just ignored them. A sample of professional advice for potential dangerous wound infections was "Just wash your hands." All wound infection documentation was sent to risk management's inconsequential files. I told one of the groups that was supposedly trying to help us, "You guys are about as worthless as tits on a boar!"

This was typical of the administration's systemic pattern of refusal to accept responsibility for our safety. Years earlier, even under my wonderful bosses, I saw a risk management report that referred to multiple assaults by patients as "inconsequential." There was a big box full of inconsequential documents with the statement "No follow-up needed"! Our patients didn't have the mental capacity to process survival instincts or ability to protect themselves. They were totally oblivious to any kind of verbal danger.

ONE WHO FLEW INTO THE CUCKOO'S NEST

Harriet's story didn't end there. This woman had a sex drive that would have put a navy company of young males, who had been out to sea for months, to shame. All we could really do was keep her in a wheelchair with a waist restraint and her hands loosely anchored to protect other patients, staff, and visitors. Well, Bill came in stating she had the right to be up and around as keeping her tied up in a wheelchair was cruel, and "She has rights." Her nurse looked at Bill and took the restraints off. I just looked at Bill and shook my head. Harriet's days on the unit weren't that unusual. I was afraid somehow; letting Harriet's loose was dangerous to the unit. I could see Bill getting us in trouble. I made a copy of that day's notes on Harriet. I was the charge nurse and could see ramifications for letting her run around loose on the unit. We didn't have enough staff for one member to stay with her all day!

Copied progress notes for Harriet:

- Scratched two staff members.
- Refused labs drawn.
- Struck out at roommate.
- Sexually inappropriate…attempting to kiss male staff.
- Remained hostile…punched male staff on the shoulder.
- Masturbating in front of staff.
- Struck female PA in back hard with fist.
- Grabbing female RN's wrist demanding, "Kiss me on the lips."
- Patient refusing medications—only able to give on emergency basis.
- Sexually preoccupied.
- Pushed the housekeeper, striking her arm.
- Attempting to kiss male staff…frequently observed in room actively masturbating.
- Lunged forward to kiss writer.
- Sexually preoccupied…pulled RN's hair yesterday…scratched PA heads while pulling hair. Forms generated for exposure. No response.
- Ran across room and accosted a dietician.

- Frequently observed manually manipulating herself.
- Tetracycline started for infection. (Note that nobody knew yet what the vaginal infections were. Also, this was about two weeks after admission. Harriet was refusing any lab work. The physician and staffs' hands were tied by patients' "rights.")
- Hit staff in the back.
- Hitting out at patients and staff.
- Struggled violently against the PA in the toilet...did not manage to scratch or strike her.
- Approached male patient and began kissing him.
- Found with male peer, kissing, lying on top of each other fully clothed...no genitalia contact.
- Frequently attempting to go into male peer's room to have "sex with him"
- Became angry at female PA and punched her in the chest and scratched her palm which broke the skin. (Forms generated for infection control. PA told there wasn't any risk.)
- Patient was found having sexual intercourse (later changed to possible intercourse) with a male patient in his room... patients separated after PA found them having intercourse.
- Clarification of "possible intercourse." Patient was straddled (legs over pelvis of male patient) and moving up and down...no physical contact observed.
- Both patients were undressed from waist down...exposure hotline was notified.

They told us they couldn't do anything unless we proved intercourse had taken place. So the day Harriet left the unit, we never knew what vaginal infectious disease Harriet might have had. It really wouldn't have mattered, because we couldn't tell one patient what illnesses another patient had. There were strict laws about patient confidentiality.

Sara came charging into the unit after Duane got hysterical about sex in the fast lane. Duane had heard from the Department of Health and was terrified of any repercussions. Sara told us to put Harriet on sexual precautions.

I just told Sara, "We don't have a protocol for sexual precautions." The best we could do was force meds and keep her anchored to a wheelchair, but Bill told us that was illegal!

"So where are these sexual precautions?" I asked. I never learned what those words were supposed to do for the patients.

Sara gave me one of those drop-dead looks. "Ginger, it's just like you. So negative."

"Yeah, Sara. How is it possible for us to protect our patients? All we get from you is verbal garbage! You and your boss are worthless. Don't you get it? You're just a laughingstock to the staff. The problem is that it isn't funny!"

Sara responded, "Just put down the words 'sexual precautions.'"

My response was "No way! Those words are meaningless, I'm not using those lies!"

Just as I thought would happen, Bill came down to the unit and started blasting us for not keeping the unit safe from Harriet. I looked at Bill and told him flat out to shut up. I showed him my copy of Harriet's chart and told him he was the one that had demanded we let Harriet out of her wheelchair. He was the one who was totally responsible for everything that happened in the unit for exposures that day. I had proof. Bill took one long look at me and walked out of the unit! I had that old sense of recurring fear go down my spine!

"Sara, I think it would better for you to talk with Bill. He told us we couldn't use what we thought would be safer precautions, the wheelchair. He claimed he had talked to the Department of Health, and they didn't think that anchoring a patient to the wheelchair was legal. Okay, Sara. Now tell me, exposures! I have and am going to use the wheelchair for patients and loose wrist restraints! The other nurses can do what they're comfortable with," I told her.

My Last Year of Work Was Emotionally Exhausting

~~~

Sara gave me one of those drop-dead looks. "Ginger, it's just like you. So negative."

My response was "I know you can't tell me about sexual precautions, because we neither have a policy nor do you have any thoughts about keeping people safe! We aren't safe and you're telling me to lie."

Sara turned to me and said, "Just put down the words 'sexual precautions.'"

"Nuh-uh! Not for me. I just can't be part of this circle of hot air!"

"Ginger, be careful. People are getting tired of your negativity, and you need your job, don't you?"

I approached Sara again asking, "What are we supposed to be doing to protect our patients and us?"

Sara's response was the same. "Ginger, be careful!"

"Sara, you don't give a damn about our patients or staff. You be careful, or you may be out of a job! Yeah, Sara, I need my job. I just want the unit to be safer. Remember you're the one that didn't want me to just do my job with the patients. You told me I had to get involved in all the self-empowerment or look for another job. Now what do you want? You want me to go back and stick my head in the sand and forget about all this political quicksand. Believe me. That's what I want to do."

"Ginger, you know the systems. Upper management thinks you're a joke. Do you think they really care? This unit has to make money and that is the objective. You'd better get that through your head."

"Sara, why does making money preclude safety? It's more than that, Sara. It's more like stupidity begetting stupidity is the goal for us. The nurses are going to take the fall for management's decisions. I've watched you hang staff out to dry one by one for bad policy. How do you sleep at night?"

Sara replied, "Ginger, I sleep very well. How do you sleep, knowing you're a joke?"

I left that showdown and went straight back to the union. After all, I had developed an extensive paper trail of unbelievable acts of violence and dangerous acts against our patients and staff. Maybe that was the biggest joke of all?

To myself, I said, "Ginger, you call yourself 'protector,' but you're more likely a fool." The reality was simple. These patients were sick outside of the unit, walking around totally unaware of the general public; nobody gets hysterical out there. There was no specific place for my patients to get mandated health care. Patients came into our unit and got some temporary physical health care; but they're in the unit with a primary diagnosis of acute psychotic illness. Then when they're clear enough for psychiatric issues, they return straight back to the street with none to very uncertain health care.

Bill called our union director and told her she had better back off our unit. Yeah, Bill, I heard you had some kind of part-time job, like treasurer or something, at the nurses' union where he was also working. So all the union nurses could do was talk about nonexistent support and say they need more of a paper trail.

Later, I read an in-house investigative report about Harriet, a new patient, and how the unit had provided patient safety by Sara, through instigation of "sexual precautions." Harriet's doctor wrote a note thinking his patient was protected by the unit policy. The doctor never learned those words had no meaning. Neither did his patient know nor did any of the other patients ever receive protection.

I felt so defeated. I knew that Duane, again the head of all the hospital nurses, was close with Bill, our unit supervisor. But I never really had the concept of power and protection that went on at those political or power levels. The Kansas part of my soul wanted to believe people still cared, no matter how power motivated they might be, and at least would want to do a good job for our patients.

"Nope! Ginger, you just flunked hospital or insurance ethics 101 for psych. Careful, you're up to your waist in this bureaucratic quicksand," I told myself. I just couldn't figure out how to back out. All I really wanted was just to take care of patients. Caring for patients kept making more sense to me.

On to the next agenda item: the legal issues. I explained there were three parts to legal problems. I only managed to get to the start of the first problem, then everything fell apart. I pushed at that time to get the old rights rewritten and put them into our new P&P book.

However, Sara at that time was saying, "Ginger, Bill is going to get all the legal things done. Don't try to confuse everybody. I'm tired of your attitude. Ginger, forget explaining anything about policies."

Now I looked at Sara and reminded her of her promise that Bill was going to do "this" and it was never done. So for the past several months, not one of our patients had a recorded understanding of their rights or lack thereof. Only some of the nurses left on Mauka unit knew patients who were involuntarily admitted. Patients that weren't actually in the world of reality had no rights. Most of these patients had no actual reality! I explained this to the group. Our patients are legally declared by law to be insane, just as if they were in a court for murder and found not responsible for the murder due to insanity! They would not go to prison. They would go to a mental hospital for care. The law recognizes that insanity means a person has no capacity to deal with reality. Plus, they have legal protection from being held responsible for criminal harmful acts to the general population due to their danger, both to self and others. They are totally without any capability for rational thoughts or behavior! We had to get three physiatrists to sign a pacific document for meds and care.

No staff could stand against this power for an extraordinary length of time. Sara's management style became even more evident—in a word *incompetent*. I noticed we, as staff, were arguing a lot. One staff would say another staff was "no good." "Sara said so." The rules for the unit changed daily. I know I was on her bad nurse list! One day, we were supposed to do one thing. The next day, it was wrong. I was getting so frustrated hearing all this crap. For me, I just kept doing my job the same way I had been trained years ago. One older male staff had the experience to recognize and articulate the turmoil we were in: "Keep the rank and file uninformed and misinformed so they can be managed by fear and confusion."

An illustration of what I am writing about is Tim. Tim, psychotic and loaded with crystal meth, arrived on the unit and promptly started a string of assaults. Bill had given us a new P&P for putting together a group of people from whom to get permission for the restraints. Bill neither identified these people nor shared how to contact them. One possibility we tried was to get Tim medicated down, but this was difficult to do over crystal meth. We can help calm a patient but usually cannot get rid of the aggressiveness without really heavily sedating, which we wouldn't do.

At least during that time we put on his walking restraints, we could get Tim up, bathed and fed. For the rest of the time, he could go to the bathroom and walk around. If we hadn't done that and followed the verbal policy, Tim would have been anchored to a bed for over fifty hours. Nobody knew who or where this "appropriate review committee" was. Waiting for a regular weekday would have meant three days of waiting. Also, even during regular workdays, we had no knowledge of who to contact.

Sara looked upset and wanted to know why we hadn't developed a behavioral plan for Tim and use our professional abilities. His nurse was nonresponsive, so I stepped in and stated that a violent, insane patient doesn't understand words like "Don't hit" or "Don't throw chairs at people" or "Don't pick up the table and toss it over…" You're going to get your lights punched out before getting three words out of your mouth!

"You guys took away all our tools to care for that patient, so what were we supposed to do?" I said. Sara gave me that back-off look. So I backed off, hearing Sara say that this too would be corrected.

When I saw Bill next, I rather harshly told him flat out, "You don't have a clue how to run this unit. We deal with the sickest of the insane patients. While you keep insisting our patients are not full-blown psychotic, most of them are totally without a drop of reality, in another word, dangerous, with emphasis on self then on others! You keep thinking of your past baseline patients, well-medicated patients."

I looked at Bill, closed my eyes, shook my head, and thought about Tim punching me in the jaw, loosening my teeth. My mind was saying, "If you don't get the hell away from me, Bill, I'll personally beat the living crap out of you."

Instead, I told Bill, "I refuse to take any more orders from you. If you want to fire me, so be it. Know this though. I will fight you and go the union if I have to!"

Now I remember, I was so angry. Yet I was so proud to work at that time with a team who was willing to take such risks. Most of us kept Tim in restraints. If we had been caught taking care of Tim, we would have risked losing our nursing licenses and each of us would have risked losing our jobs. We knew this was gross insubordination. As a team, we sat together and talked about it. We concluded that Bill had once again changed the unit's policy without any formal education for staff, and he had not bothered to produce a new policy and procedure (P&P) for the unit's manual, at least none that we had seen. We would operate according to the written standard, which had been Flo's. Not all the staff was on board with this, but they kept quiet, and I took over as Tim's nurse. We regained some good patient care.

Staff were really a little encouraged by this concentrated patient's volley of assaults. Each assault was written up on an incident form, then sent to the hospital's risk management. In risk management, Lynda, the department head, was to review the event forms for legal potential and also for safety. Several weeks later, I reviewed the outcome of her assessment. It was one of our very assaultive patients—assaults were where I learned a medication error rated more action than people being assaulted. All our assault forms were in the inconsequential box! In other words, when action from anywhere was needed, ignore the incident form!

I should have known better. After all, I had fought Lynda's insistence on remaining ignorant for some time. Lynda never cared about true safety issues. Her focus was to look at potential lawsuits involving the hospital. I told Sara that Bill was totally ignorant about caring for our patients. Also, he was a threat to the patients getting good care! Walking restraints were still legal. All those assaults would not have happened, except for Bill's insistences that we couldn't use restraints. I didn't tell anybody I used walking restraints.

"No, Bill isn't like that, Ginger." Sara continued, "Bill has worked so hard for the unit, and he is trying so hard to bring order to the unit. You seem to have some unwarranted personal feelings about Bill, and it gets in the way."

My response was "Yes, I do have a lot of personal feelings about Bill. Well, doggone, anyhow! I had been charged once and knew what it was like to get grilled and prosecuted."

Frustration Plus Lawsuit Charges

A few years back, one of my more brilliant psychotic patients had sued me and another nurse. According to him, this lawsuit was about illegally giving him forced medication. Another psychiatrist hadn't seen the signed medication consent and confirmed to Henry, the patient, that, yes, he had been given medication illegally. So I had to sit and review the charges against me. Luckily for Lynda in risk management and myself, I found the signed med consent. The hospital, the physician, and I were covered. Without that lousy one piece of paper, Henry as his own lawyer would have destroyed our careers and made a lot of money. He fought all the way to the State Supreme Court while he was still completely paranoid and delusional. Yet he had a really brilliant legal mind!

Along with Henry's med issue, he charged me with a forced medication on him. Henry's main medication was Lithium. I was required to go before a board (don't remember what kind), and Henry, acting as a prosecuting attorney, started on me by saying, "Ginger, you told me if I didn't take my Lithium pill, you were going to give me a shot!" I told them that wasn't true. Then he asked me how I could remember from so long ago and so many patients in between. I told him and the board the only way I could force meds was by shots. There were no shots for Lithium as Lithium came in pills only. I couldn't cram a pill down his throat. That stopped the whole proceedings. I was told to go home. Never heard any more about it!

Sad, because without any medication, Henry would stay psychotic. Those of us involved could see the illness, but we had no way to help Henry. The courts were responding to him as if he were a rational human being and acted accordingly. He managed to get a lot of people in trouble. Henry claimed there was a conspiracy between the judges, the lawyers, Sears, FBI, CIA, and doctors. According to Henry, he had very powerful allies, even if they were from outer space. I read out of one of his many legal briefs to the court. Henry had written that Onus, as an impartial outer space council, was likely to say, "We of the Lodestar Cosmic Command Council, having read the briefs of the appellant and appellees, offer the following concise opinion…Nurses are still liable for administering inappropriate medicine…that audiotape information came from a psychic about the subjects…but were looking for voice identification so that, behind the scenes, pressure could be applied to the voices not to any statements contrary to a brainwashing manipulation plot…It is the council's conclusion that there is probable cause to believe that a brainwashing manipulation plot overriding the rules and principles and application of law is going on, which is so pervasive, it isn't necessary for the various Circuit Court judges to have been in contact with one another…Finally, we of the Lodestar Cosmic Command Council conclude…"

Henry kept this legal tennis ball going for years. One piece of paper, correctly done medication consent, was all that stood between being a paid nurse and a financially destroyed ex-nurse. I still wonder what happened to Henry when all his legal moves were done. I feel it was the only thing that kept him from violence.

The reason he had been brought into the hospital originally was violence toward his mother and father; they were terrified of him. To this day, I always suspected Henry might try to kill somebody.

Anybody whom he felt could challenge him. Anyway, in my mind, I was very aware of the legal importance of good medication consents. The new policy, as Bill wrote it and sneaked the policy in, was about not forcing meds on patients into the policy book. He never said anything about it to the nurses. I ran across that new policy, tore it out of the policy book, and took it down to Bill's office.

Bill had developed a medication policy that only a rational human could sign without any contingency. It was not for a psychotic patient who was disabled or unable even to understand his illness. It was like telling a surgeon he could not do emergency head surgery on an unconscious patient until the patient could sign the paperwork.

I then went to VP Rutt and told him what I had done and why. VP Rutt, shaking his head, asked me if I wanted him to try to talk to Duane. But Duane wasn't in his line of authority; however, maybe he could help by talking. My response was yes. I never would have made it without VP Rutt!

My last legal thrust was when Bill once again started a new restraint policy. I told the group that Sara had claimed to the union that this was done some time ago. That was all lies and I said so. Sara blurted out, "Ginger, when will you learn not to say anything that isn't couched in politically correct terms?" My statement caused a ten-minute fight about the political differences between lies and truth. Got past that.

For problems with the restraint policy, we still had two conflicting policies on the unit, and nobody knew what we were supposed to do. I later told the staff I was staying with the old policy.

Sara confronted me in the meeting with "Ginger? Everybody else I talked to seemed to know what he or she was supposed to do. Maybe you just need to look harder?"

I just smiled and said, "Okay, Sara, I might be wrong. In the restraint policy, it states, an appropriate committee comprised of… professionals, as well as by an external psychiatrist not involved with the patient care…are supposed to review various degrees of restraints. Sara, who are these people? I need to meet them."

Bill jumped in here. "Ginger, there is a committee."

Darn him anyhow. I was kind of enjoying this. I said no. He basically told me to stop tormenting Sara and told Sara he would be giving her clarification shortly. I looked over at Sara and told her about the times we had been forced to use walking restraints behind their backs because it was neither forbidden nor was there a clear policy. So far, it was only their upper management's say-so. Sara wasn't thrilled. I asked what we were supposed to do with extremely violent patients. We didn't have padded rooms. It was too cruel to keep patients tied down, and we couldn't let them up without one-on-one security, so what choice did we have? We had to put walking restraints on them.

Infection control was a hot topic. Everything else was more legally oriented. Infection issues were our bodies' danger points. For this issue, Sara took it upon herself to write and send it up to her bosses the guidelines for the isolation of pulmonary tuberculosis, which states that patients with active or suspected TB must be admitted or transferred to a private room and isolated.

Sara, along with Bill, said that we never had any potential TB infections on our unit. Sara said at the start of the meeting, "Ginger, you know our policy about TB isolation." In other words, she just wrote up a whole bunch of lies. As far as she was concerned, by lying about our infection control, we were automatically safe. We no longer had to worry about infection control.

"Yes, Sara, I know what is supposed to happen. Maybe you can explain to me why we have three patients in our unit right now: one with a positive TB test, one of whom we are having to run a skin test for possible active TB, and another just came in with an old TB diagnosis. To my knowledge, none of them have had a chest X-ray ordered. One of those patients is running around spitting green phlegm and coughing in everybody's face, not to mention she has taken a few bites out of people. Which law shall we break? The wheelchair or the just accept the fact other patients or staff are just going to get infected?"

Here in the meeting, I was asked if there were any other issues. I briefly looked at Lynda from risk management and told her what I had said many years ago. "Don't hold our unit to a different medical standard than the rest of the hospital."

Lately, we have been having more and more medically complicated patients. I noted that when we had our last death on the unit, we had to go the whole nine yards through a coroner inquest and review the staff for criminal charges. It's hard enough to deal with a medical or psychotic patient without having to look over your shoulder, wondering when you were going to get charged for homicide. Lynda once again stated her famous words: "Ginger, people aren't supposed to die on a psych unit." I looked across at Lynda and knew she had long since forgotten Mr. Y and had no idea what I was even talking about. Nobody else in the room knew either, so this issue died. I would have to be content if we could just get the main concerns worked through.

After a short time, nothing much had changed. Lu from infection control came up for a meeting with the staff. Lu still hung on to her delusional ways. At one point, a PA mentioned his frustration with taking a patient down, scratching, biting, spitting while on the floor then having security come through the door after putting on their plastic gloves. For us, it was all over; the damage was done. Lu laughed, then repeated her smart-ass remark, "We could encase you all in plastic."

My response was "Lu, do you even care about the staff or patients? Why do you call yourself a nurse, when you don't care?" So more time goes by. I got a call from the OB floor. A new mother with a new baby needed to come down to one of our isolation rooms. She had TB. I told her she couldn't come down to our unit. First, we didn't have an isolation room, and second, our patients required a major psychiatric diagnosis. She thanked me and hung up.

After that long infection control meeting took place, everything got dropped. No medication consent clarifications. No change in the restraint policy. Patients continued not to have their rights given to them. Of course, eight out of ten coming through the door wouldn't have been able to sit still long enough to hear their rights, let alone understand them. Patients with previously known MRSA infections were running around the unit.

I asked a patient's doctor to check a wound. His response could have echoed my own thoughts. "Why? What would change? She has been in here off and on for some time. She is an alcoholic, and her wounds aren't going to get treated, and nobody is going to follow-up on any exposures." He was right.

Then with a big sigh, he said, "Take me to her and I'll take care of her wound."

Our Happier Ending! Yeah!

~~~~~~~~~~~~~~~~~~

On one of my last nights on the unit, I was standing near a patient's door. Suddenly, I had arms wrapped around me and was picked up from behind. I immediately recognized a voice loudly hollering, "Gina, Gina, you're here!" I immediately knew that voice. She was my old patient who I had cared for many times over the years. She always called me by her nickname for me, Gina.

She dropped me to the floor. I turned around and we hugged each other. I asked, "Why are you here? You're not sick, Tiny?"

"No, Gina, I'm taking my medicine. I came in to help my son." Tonight, she was here to visit her son who was newly diagnosed as a manic. He was so angry, just like his mother had been. Now Tiny and I were like long lost sisters. I had seen her children visit many times. She would be extremely helpful to me in understanding her son's feelings. Tonight, we would work together to get her son under control. I went out with Tiny and met her children and grandchildren. We hugged. Yeah, Tiny, a lot of our life had been spent together.

Tiny told me, "Gina, finally, I could stop being so angry about my illness. Now I take my medication and stopped fighting everybody."

"Tiny, your son is lucky to have a mama like you. You will help him start accepting his illness."

Again, I told Tiny, "Your son is so lucky to have a mama like you. He will do fine, because you will make him take his meds, right?"

Tiny laughed and said, "Yes, Gina!" We hugged and said our goodbyes.

This all brought back the first time I met Tiny twelve years ago. I was working the graveyard shift by myself and one staff member. Because our second staff was sent down to ER after a patient hit him, we had only two staff on the Mauka unit. This was my first encounter with Tiny, and she was one angry biting, hitting female manic. Walking into her room, I saw she was restrained to her bed, and she had gotten herself all tangled up in the loose restraints. While screaming, she wanted to go to the bathroom. I tried to call the Makai unit, but no answer. Everybody over there must be out on the floor. So I sent my PA over to Makai, telling him to bring over several more staff as we needed help. They could finish what they were doing because our patient was contained.

Well, that was not quite the way it went down. I approached Tiny, not realizing she had one arm free. Tiny was furious and grabbed me, pulling me on top of her on my back and started chewing on my clothed shoulder. It seemed like forever, but at last, staff came through the door, and we got Tiny anchored. I got some more meds for her. She fell asleep, and we released her to her waist and one arm restraint. Tiny fought her illness for many years. I had watched her children grow up. She hadn't been in the unit for at least a year. It was a wonderful gift to see her one last time.

My last two weeks on the unit became remarkably interesting. I arrived at work and staff rushed me with "Have you heard?"

My response was "Heard what?"

"Ginger, Sara's gone."

She had a meeting, and when she came back, all she said was, "I've got another job in the hospital. I'm not your boss anymore!" Whoa, what happened there?

The staff went on to say, "Bill has quit and will be working full time at the nurses' union. He won't be here anymore!"

My first response was "Wow! Well, I'll be damned!" Nobody knew what had happened.

Although that last year, I had gone and found Vice President Dan Rutt. He was VP of the whole hospital. The first time I busted into his office in tears about Juan and the loss of lives on the unit. I was so desperate. Mr. Rutt listened to me expressing concerns and told me he wanted me to feel free to talk to him anytime. He wanted to know what was happening in Kekela. I was a frequent flyer, and he was such a kind person. I always felt better. He made me feel safe, like my brother did. At the end, I poured my heart out, he listened as usual, shaking his head, and asked me if I wanted him to try and talk to Duane. Duane wasn't in his line of authority; however, maybe he could help by talking. My response was yes. I never would have made it without VP Rutt! This is the first time I ever told anybody about Mr. Rutt helping me. I never saw Mr. Rutt again after that last time, but he was a real gift that last year on the unit!

I was just blown away. All I could think of was somebody well above my pay grade had had enough. Our psychiatrists had been getting very upset over their patients not getting medications. Their patients required our unit because they were too sick to be outside. They had not been taking their Lithium. So they were admitted to our unit to get enough shots or oral medications into them, in addition to their mainstay medication, Lithium. There were no shots for Lithium. We had used other medications to calm them down. While getting them back on to their main medication, Lithium, which most of them had stopped taking, they usually thought they got rid of their illness, and ergo, they did not need their medication anymore. Many of our patients were living on the streets and couldn't get medication or their medication was stolen. Bill could not or refused to recognize this concept in our patients. He had no idea what it was like for our patients who had to live on the streets.

Dr. Bernice Coleman, chief of psychiatry, and I worked together for years. She scared some of the nurses as she was very straightforward and no-nonsense. She thought what was happening on the unit was unnecessary and destructive. We liked each other and had many talks about what was happening in the unit. I think among the psychiatrists, Coleman, and of course, my silent lifeline, VP Rutt, must have done something to save the unit. For the rest of the day, I was in shock! Then the reality of what this meant for my Kekela, which I loved, sunk in, and I felt completely happy.

I want to stop here and be clear regarding the administration that gave us back our Kekela and exactly what that meant to me. The Queen's Hospital administration, in my eyes, showed and let us know, Kekela and staff, how much they cared about all of us. My admiration and wonderment of Queen's administration fills me with such pride and respect for our patients and work. I am just overwhelmed at the chance to have had the experience of working for Queen's in their dedication to quality of care.

Here is where I left my wonderful years of working and learning to care for high-acuity patients. Now as I am reliving all my years on my unit, somewhere over twenty-five years later, with only about a year that was difficult due to the bureaucratic administration, not the patients. Now I have a more reflective mindset about that last year. The new management did not understand the acuity of our patients. Today, this is, I'm thinking, an ongoing problem, not at Queen's Hospital but throughout many other hospitals or institutions throughout the USA. Acute psychotic care is nowhere close to general mental illness. Only people who have done the work with acute psychotic patients should be allowed to develop plans or programs for acutely psychotic patients. Anything less than having that experience leads to extremely poor care for a lot of mentally ill people, along with the extreme danger for the staff that takes care of acute psychotic patients who truly need professional and loving care.

I can honestly say I am not even close to understanding all the distinct types of mental illnesses there are. I am only very confident in my own world of experience of highly acute psychotic patients. I empathize with these patients; this is where all my learning took place.

All the new management's experience was extremely limited in dealing with acute psychotic illnesses. Their whole body of mental illness was for more "normal" mental illnesses, which means they dealt with highly functioning patients. The rules of care are vastly different and one example of that would be the first patient's rights! A highly functioning person has a lot more rights because they are more competent to discuss their illness and understand their own needs, wants, and rights. The majority of my highly psychotic, sick patients had no rational capabilities. The last year of my work will give you an example of the rift which took place in our unit. New bureaucratic management and staff clashed frequently over how to care for a highly acute psychotic patient. New managements had an utter lack of knowledge about how to care for acute patients' needs. This is what happens in the real world of our own country's lack of understanding about the good and bad aspects of quality patient care. I ask the lawmakers to rethink some laws, like restraint usage. They are for safety and have absolutely nothing to do with punitive care!

The new management's unwillingness to learn about the many differences between the truly psychotic and relative dysfunctional caused us terrible suffering. By their ignorance, they were driven to turn our unit into one of their relatively comfortable, rational, and profitable units. Our patients could not suddenly be expected to be well enough to sit down as rational people and start talking about their illness. They weren't anywhere close enough to the baseline ability to think.

I will give the new management's depth of knowledge about how to deal with rational patients far superior to mine. I had no experience with rational patients and wouldn't have a clue about how to care for them. All my care knowledge was for patients who were dangerous to themselves and others. These patients were incapable of caring for themselves, such as their needs to sleep, eat, bathe, dress, or find a toilet. Many of these patients just lashed out at nothing. Their minds are overtaken at times by an exploding morass of violent conflicting or delusional thoughts! Our care was very specific to these patients' needs.

Now all these years later, when I talk about my work, people frequently ask me, "How many security guards did you have on the unit?"

I would look at them and say, "None!" We never had guards in the unit. There was not enough time to get the hospital's security guards up to our unit. Our unit eruptions happened in a matter of seconds, not minutes. We always had to respond in split seconds. Guards would have needed three to five minutes to respond, and we didn't have those minutes! The guards were all over the hospital, plus they had to take an elevator up one floor to our unit. There were no stairs. Everybody would have had to wait for security. We would have had to wait anywhere from maybe up to three to four minutes or longer. By then all the damage, along with patients, staff, and visitors getting hurt, would have been horrific. Security wasn't standing outside our door waiting.

The average height of our personnel was about five feet five inches to five feet ten inches. We had three male staff over six feet, but those guys weren't always around for us on the floor. We had to mobilize in a second and could do a takedown of a wild patient within a couple of seconds, using our floor staff numbers. With restraints, we could have them under control and heading back to their room within a couple of minutes. Remember, if we just used four to six staff, we had over five to nine hundred pounds of weight to take down a patient. Even when we had only two to three staff, we had usually about three to over found hundred pounds. That much weight running into a patient, hitting them on the waist and legs, will knock them off their feet.

For the most part, our scary takedowns happened to male patients and occasionally to a female. I can say we never had a takedown result in any injury to a patient. No takedown ever required the patient having to go down to the ER or an ER physician having to come up to the unit. In fact, it was the other way around. It was always the staff that had to go down to the ER. I take that back. I had one patient go down for new arm pain. He came back okay, just pulled a muscle. Staff usually came back to the unit cleared enough to finish their shift.

For females, when they went wild, with as few as three staff, we could usually grab their arms and haul them back to their room and get them into waist restraints. There were a few females who were wild fighters, and they really fought hard.

Here is where I want the public to try understanding that when they make laws for mentally ill patients, one can't just group all mentally ill patients together under one law. Patients' rights vary. When some people say using leather restraints for one set of mentally ill patients is cruel, you must think, "What is the real level of illness for needing restraints?" Walking restraints work very well for acute psychotic patients when they wake up. That is a safety feature for getting the patient up freely walking around and not dangerous to other patients or staff or visitors. They can sit down and eat and perform all their daily ADLs, activities of daily living, or routine needs. We stopped the walking restraints as soon as we assess any patient will not get violent. It takes a different number of days for psychotic medication Lithium to work! As soon as Lithium can calm the brain centers and compartmentalize irrational thoughts safely, we consider them close enough to baseline. Then we can transfer them to our less restrictive unit, Makai, for longer-term needs. Usually by then, they can talk and comprehend more reasonably.

I have shared my experiences in a vastly different world of psychotic illness than one in which many American people have even heard of. Anybody with a family member who has an acute psychotic illness diagnosis will understand the differences between normal mental problems and acute psychotic problems. Many have had to live pure lives of Pure Hell! Yes, they know the extreme differences in insanity problems. The book *One Flew Over the Cuckoo's Nest* showed and spoke only to mental problems that could be verbally worked with. Some meds work for comparatively minor problems like anxiety, loss of temper, depression, and run-of-the-mill personality disorders. My story is caring for patients who "flew into the cuckoo's nest!" I have very deep feelings for these lost human beings and their families.

Comparing Guam's Care to America's Care

When I went to Guam and worked there for about a year and a half, I was shocked by their care for psychotic patients. Guam puts America to shame. Guam was the epitome of caring for their psychotic people. Their acute unit was in an old hospital. They were building a new hospital and were getting ready to add a psychiatric addition. In the meantime, we were using the old falling-apart hospital. I could not even recognize what I was seeing when I walked into the unit. I saw a staff lounging on a sofa and what looked like four possible patients. I asked the psych aid what the patient count was. He told me they had four patients. After a quick assessment of the patient's status, it was obvious they were totally at baseline and ready to be discharged. That is about the totality of how the next year and a half went.

Guam had housing for their psychotic mentally ill people. The housing was made up of apartments. They had staffing for each building. I never got into the nuts and bolts of their care. The care was top-notch! I did know that. They had transportation for shopping, the beach, and appointments. It was wonderful. For all the time I was there, I never had one takedown of a patient. That was amazing to me. It was wonderful, and I never saw a full-blown psychotic patient!

The biggest thing we had with one of the older female patients was a funeral or a wedding. The staff fixed her hair and got her all dressed up. The psych aid got all dressed up and escorted her to the event in his own car, bringing her back hours later. For Christmas, our local Chamorro nurse, who worked in the unit, would shut down the entire unit, load up the patients, and take them to her home for a big Christmas dinner. That unit was like a great big family! Many times, the unit was shut down to allow for an afternoon at the beach, which was very close.

One time, when I came into the unit, I saw the staff getting somebody up out of restraints. I asked, "What happened?"

The staff's response, "Oh, a tourist came in and it got pretty wild. So they brought the tourist here. We medicated him, and he is returning home today." That was pretty much the height of excitement I ever saw in Guam. Everybody got to watch a lot of TV.

Guam, this little island out in the ocean, maintains acute psychotic people like they were real human beings. Guam had the heart for psychotic patients, who couldn't totally care for themselves. I can't say what it's like today but doubt they have changed their feelings about caring for people who are mentally ill. They understand that without care, mentally ill patients can't function on their own. With help, they can have nice and safe lives.

Then I came back to Queen's and to a very uncaring America toward the mentally ill. I was so ashamed of my country! When the US government shut down all the insane asylums and dumped patients out on the street with the promise of setting up clinics, the money was cut, which resulted in way too few clinics.

Today, way too many mentally ill people are street people throughout our country. The only words given to the sick people dumped out of the institutions were "Sorry, you're on your own now. Good luck." Ever since then, all that meant was "So sorry to hear about your life. Don't call us. We'll call you!"

Families can only care for their sick only as long as patients take their meds. These patients without their meds are dangerous to people, televisions, furniture, refrigerators, and anything they can lay their hands on! American political bodies like our federal government need to set up a whole new system of caring for these people! They have done nothing!

I say to our Federal Government's Senators and Representatives, "Shame on you!"

I ask the people of America to give some thought to this. We need to have a long-lasting tsunami of phone calls to our federal house and senate people to push for caring for our insane or psychotic mentally ill people. When you're out and about and see an insane or psychotic mentally ill person, you notice and look the other way to try to avoid them. Instead, stop for just a minute and look at them. Then go home, get your congressperson and senator on speed dial, and ask them what they have done today to correct the lack of care that our acute mentally ill human beings aren't getting.

From the US Department of Health and Human Services

———∽———

Below is a report on mentally ill people, a report that I found interesting! I want to thank the readers for reading my story. Please think of these tormented human beings, so much in need of care and safety. The majority of them can't make it on their own, through no fault of their own. Please, please! Help these people!

The US Department of Health and Human Services reports that one in five Americans has experienced issues with mental health; and one in ten youth have suffered a major bought of depression.

The effects of mental illness on life quality of life and health outcomes are significant. Individuals with severe mental illness such as schizophrenia, major depressive disorder, or bipolar disorder (about four percent of the population) live on average 25 years less than other Americans. As many as a third of individuals with a serious diagnosis do not receive any consistent treatment.

The mentally ill are far more likely to be the victims of violent crime rather than the perpetrators. Only 3-5% of violent crimes can be tied in some way to a person's mental illness, and people with mental illnesses are ten times more likely to be the victims of violence than the general public.

And while the relationship between mental illness and poverty is complicated, having a severe mental illness increases the likelihood of living in poverty. According to some estimates, a quarter of homeless Americans are seriously mentally ill.

Most troubling, perhaps, is the criminalization of mental illness in the United States. At least a fifth of all prisoners in the United States have a mental illness of some kind, and between 25 and 40 percent of mentally ill people will be incarcerated at some point in their lives.

A study by Human Rights Watch revealed that prison guards routinely abuse mentally ill prisoners. Darren Rainey, a mentally ill prisoner at the Dade Correctional Institution in Florida, was boiled to death in a shower after being locked in it for more than two hours by prison guards.

More are sent to prison in part because fewer mental health facilities are available. The disappearance of psychiatric hospitals and asylums is part of the long-term trend toward "deinstitutionalization." But jails and prisons have taken their place. Today, the largest mental health facilities in the United States are the Cook County

Jail, the Los Angeles County Jail, and Rikers Island.

The effects of mental illness on life quality of life and health outcomes are significant. Individuals with severe mental illness such as schizophrenia, major depressive disorder, or bipolar disorder (about four percent of the population)

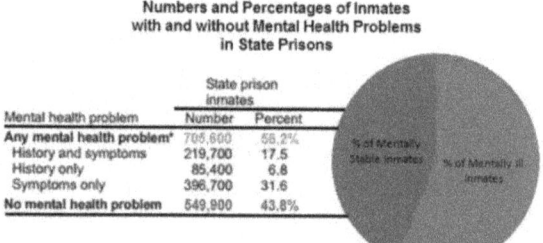

Darren Rainey, who suffered from schizophrenia, died in 2012 from burns to over ninety percent of his body after prison guards locked him in a shower for two hours with 180°F water (left). A graph and chart showing the percentage of inmates with and without mental health problems in state prisons in 2006 (right).

Taken from the Miami Herald, part of the McClatchy Media Network on Florida Prisons, "Miami-Dade State Attorney Katherine Fernandez Rundle's office revealed that, after a five-year legal dispute, no charges will be filed against the four prison guards who allegedly tortured and killed Darren Rainey. In addition, the four accused guards will be allowed to keep their jobs as Florida correctional officers. Prosecutors concluded that Rainey's death was an "accident"... Some consider this an obvious cover-up.

The family of Darren Rainey has settled a civil rights lawsuit against the state of Florida and others for $4.5 million, the Miami Herald learned. The deal came nearly six years after Rainey's death, which was all but ignored by authorities until 2014—when the Miami Herald wrote about it as part of a three-year investigation into the abuse and suspicious deaths of inmates in the Florida Department of Corrections.

I looked back at the unit thirty-eight years later. So many patients, so much learning. Then when I lost my bosses of many years, I was consumed by the bureaucratic quicksand, knowing my time had come. I had walked into that Kansas River with its shifting administrative quicksand, knowing I was seeing my last view of me in a former world of caring for my psychotic patients. I was exhausted and had become worthless to my patients. By my side were all the boxes of paper trails that had been developed over so many years. They would go with me. They had been worth nothing, except to me. On the riverbank, I caught one last glimpse of all the new staff who were being led by new administrations to come into the river's quicksand. They couldn't see me as I slipped under the water. I wondered if they even knew about the shifting bureaucratic quicksand. I had stepped into that quicksand. I fought the quicksand and won for the moment. Then looking at today's mental health, I realize I lost. No one person can fix this broken system. It must be done by our government and Americans seeing, thinking, and talking about these destitute people and standing up for them!

Ugh! Patients and Physicians Are Robots

When I came back to the American mainland in about 1996, all my life until then, I've always had private doctors. I didn't go to a doctor for about ten years until I moved to a small town in upper Minnesota, sometime around 2010. Right now, I am an old lady looking at today's 2024 American health care. The USA medical health care is atrocious, devastating, and makes me furious. You're not getting practicing physicians. You're getting walking, talking policy and procedures, P&P, robots from hostage insurances making robotic physicians. Physicians are unable to freely practice medicine. Insurance companies have also made P&P robotic care in hospitals and staff. I can only speak for two states seeking health care, so I can't speak for the whole country. But if you recognize what I'm saying, then include yourself in my experience. Repeating myself, you're getting walking, talking policy and procedure robots. These robotic physicians are completely unable to use hard-learned skills or compassion for their patients. That reality for me is really, absolutely unbelievable, yet it's true!

This was what I had to learn the hard way. I had a simple bladder infection. I called my doctor and was told I had to see my doctor. I hollered at that, "No, I just need to go to a lab and pee into a cup." The response was "No, you have to see your doctor first."

I saw my doctor and blew up! He told me he had to follow P&P. The P&P says you must see a doctor before, and then you can pee in a cup.

I told him, "You're the doctor. You just give the order."

His reply, "Nope, you have to see the doctor first. I have to follow P&P."

I asked him how bad this was and continued, "You're not allowed to practice medicine, what you trained for years and years? Then you swore to the Hippocratic oath about caring for patients?"

My doctor told me that it's really bad! "Physicians no longer have the right to practice medicine," he told me. Later on, I heard from where this all came, the hospital management. The evil words *insurance companies* have total control over our health care! I haven't researched that. I'm only repeating the words I've heard.

You can't fight it! Insurances, according to the administrators with whom I talked, said that insurances control what hospitals can and can't do. Completely ignorant about generating P&Ps for hospital staff, a multitude of P&Ps are made. So I asked, in that office visit, if that meant the staff also have to be walking, talking P&P robots. His head was down, and the most sorrowful face stared back at me without a response.

I looked at my doctor and told him to just watch me. "I'm gonna fight this, at least I'm going to try."

He told me with a sad look, "Good luck."

I wrote a letter (see below) to the hospital (Riverwood Healthcare Center, Aitkin, Minnesota). They sent me back a letter, asking me to come in to talk regarding my concern. That intervention went very well. They gave me a special nurse that I could call when I had a medical problem, when I didn't want to see my physician but needed medical care. That was a great gift!

My Letter

―――∞―――

September 19, 2018
To Whomever Deals With Policy and Procedure Concerns:

A little history first. In 1984 I was working in Meeker County Hospital Litchfield, MN when the first wave of restricting practicing physicians hit. It was named DRG's, insurance companies, telling physicians how long patients could stay in the hospital, no regards for patients' needs or physicians' assessments. Thousands of hospitals were affected. Inpatient numbers dropped dramatically with thousands of nurses and staff being laid off. The insurance companies' profits went through the roof. DRG's had nothing to do with health care.

Suddenly, finding myself here in MN, now I discovered, to my dismay, what had happened to getting physician care today in MN. Discovering the second wave of insurances restricting practicing physicians of their rights to hold up their duty to the Hippocratic Oath, I had been living in HI for ten years and ten years in S.D. In HI I had a private doctor and in S. D. I never went to a doctor. I found an outstanding physician, Dr. Burgos. Then I found out from Dr. Burgos, in whom I have the greatest confidence and respect, that he is required to follow Policy and Procedures (P&P). Then, a simple bladder infection became a very complicated procedure!

My first bladder infection in MN went like this. I called Dr. Burgos and talked with his nurses asking for a lab and med order. She informed me that I had to come in and see the doctor. I thought this absolutely bizarre for a simple bladder infection! I argued, "I am seventy-three years old and never had to see a doctor for a bladder infection." She said that's not the way the hospital P&P works. He can't give you orders for lab or meds without seeing him. I'm still in shock over hearing that! So, I made the appointment for two days later and followed the P&P, griping the whole way. I told Dr. Burgos. "I trust you. I don't have a clue, nor do I care about hospital's P&P and I'm not sure I like being under the care of or even the idea of a one size fits all P&P book caring for me!" Burgos was very good with me, but firmly repeated he had to follow P&P! He told me I could go to urgent care the next time, which might simplify my needs.

Having a bowel issue, I went through several bladder infections. So, the next infection, with a very wary eye, I went to Hospital through their full Urgent Care two hours and twenty-five-minute routine, then stopped off at CVS pharmacy to pick up my meds. Took another forty-five minutes to wait for the order. After over three hours since leaving my home, got my meds and started heading for home, my anger level was boiling, along with feeling sick, crying and extremely upset. The girls that dealt with me were wonderfully good and very understanding, while I was having a lot of trouble controlling my anger.

Your P&Ps don't have anything to do with patients' wants, needs, care or time. It is strictly used as a way toward the Hospital's money-making business interest. After another round of P&P examples, I think you should never ever use the phrase this Hospital cares about their patients. You've made my physician your own personal one size fits all P&P money-making robot for the hospital. You have suffocated any chance for my physician to operate independently with all his years and years of training, knowledge and ability to care for his patients!

I have hit the wall on getting a physician that I so desperately wanted, Dr. Burgos' whom I trust, respect, along with his complete integrity. I was so excited and relieved when I met him and thought, as I approach the end stage of my life, together he'll help me feel safe walking down this unknown path with him. You're P&Ps I don't trust, and I feel like they are an enemy to any kind of care for me. So, you must tell me how to proceed. Whomever is responsible for P&P, you need to have that person sit down with me and talk with me! Now when I'm with Burgos, we're fine. But as soon as I hear the words *have to follow P&P*, I shut down and want to go home. The whole visit is no longer safe!

Virginia (Ginger) Pendo, RN (BSN)

That worked out great as the next bladder infection went like this. I called my nurse, told her I had another bladder infection. I wanted a standing order with the lab to test for a bladder infection.

She said, "I'll talk to the doctor."

I responded, "Then call me back."

My nurse called back. He told her that there would be a standing order for the lab. This all took place on a Friday. It was so late; I would go in on Saturday.

On Saturday, I called into the lab in the afternoon, knowing labs are usually really busy in the morning. The lab tech answered, and when I told her who I was, she interrupted me, saying, "Boy, I want to meet you. You've caused quite a stir down here. I really want to meet you."

Okay, I asked her if she was busy.

"Yeah, I'm reading a really good book right now, but come on in. I'll stop reading for you." We both laughed. I could tell she was an older tech.

So I left home and went straight to the hospital. This was fun. I stopped at check-in and was told I didn't have an appointment. Told her I have a standing order. She said that she had never heard of a standing order and would have to call the lab. Well, the lab girl said she'd be right up to get me. She came up, and we went down laughing the whole way. That check-in girl sat there with her mouth open, sputtering, "She hasn't got an appointment." I urinated in the cup and went home.

Well, my now practicing doctor and I had some good years together. He was thrilled. I told him, "You doctors shouldn't put up with this shit." Told him to tell his other doctors (because he had told me the P&P stuff made the doctors frustrated and angry) go get a set of balls and for the female doctors go get on their high horses! Fight back. You have to fight this. You're physicians. You're smart. You work so hard to become a practicing doctor. Don't lose that. Your patients are depending on you practicing your medicine.

When in Kansas, I had a rude awakening. Not too long ago, I had to go in for a procedure. After I completed the procedure, which was pretty extensive, I was in the recovery area. The procedure was done, and the nurse said I could get dressed and go home. Okay, that was good for me. I had had it with policy and procedures, so I told the nurse that I'll be glad to get out of there. I called a cab to get home, and I wanted to get out of that building to sit. I had brought my own folded-up chair so I could sit outside. It was a sun-shining, beautiful day.

Nope, the nurses said I had to wait in the waiting area as that was the P&P area. I told them, "No, I'm going to sit outside the waiting room door."

They told me if I did that, I would be discharged AMA, against medical advice, and insurance would not pay for my procedure. I asked where the doctor was to give me that advice. I was told there was no doctor needed.

I got dressed, got off the gurney, picked up my stuff, and started to head out of the room. Suddenly, four nurses were standing in front of me. I asked them, "Are you nurses?"

They answered yes, and one of them added that she was the charge nurse.

I looked at them and told them, "I'm a real nurse! You're not nurses. You're walking, talking P&P robots!" I shoved past them and got to the door.

As I reached for the handle, one nurse who had followed me grabbed my hand. I looked at her and asked, "Are you going to fight me? I'm a seventy-eight-year-old woman."

She looked at me and grabbed my chair. "Well, I'm going to take you out there and set you down!" I just turned my head and followed, smiling. She watched me through the door window. The cab arrived, the driver helped me get my stuff, got into the car, and off we went.

Those kinds of events let me know where our modern medical reality is. The public is being molded into walking, talking P&P patient robots. One lady shopper in a Walgreen's store was talking in a very upset way to a pharmacist. We went out of the store together. I told her I was an old nurse and asked her, "What's going on?"

She explained that her mother, in her late eighties, had good cognition and desperately wanted cataracts removed from her eyes as she could barely see. The doctor had told her she had something in her neck that required surgery and that she couldn't have cataract surgery until she had the neck surgery. The doctor told her this was P&P, and there wasn't anything he could do. Without this neck procedure, insurance would not pay for her cataract surgery.

Her mother already had quite a few surgeries and didn't want another surgery. She had clearly refused this surgery. She said, "I've had enough, but please let me have eyesight. I'd like to be able to see, with what time I have left."

Her daughter was crying, beside herself. I told her she might talk to insurance people and see if they would give an exemption to her mother or go get a lawyer. She said they couldn't afford a lawyer, but she'd try the insurance people. I wished her luck! Physicians just roll over. I don't know why they don't fight. Patients aren't real anymore; patients are just robots. Nobody who's alive can get the care of a physician who can use their own hard work and skills! Nobody's human anymore!

My mother was a woman reared from parents who were reared in 1800s. At a very young age of eight, she knew she would fight for the rest of her life for women's freedom, and she did. I admired her for close to forty-plus years of work she put into that. But most of all, I loved her with all my heart. Finally, in the late 1960s, she started receiving recognition for her body of knowledge. That was her gift to women.

The last gift of wisdom my mother gave me was at the end of her life. She told me what the biggest thing she learned was about ignorance. In her words, she explained, "Honey, know this. Everybody is ignorant. Let me explain. I spent my life studying everything I could. At the end, I realized if you were standing on a whole beach of sand, with each grain of sand holding a body of knowledge. Then when I leave this earth, all the knowledge I learned in one lifetime would be like bending over and picking up one pinch of the sand with my fingers and claiming that one pinch is all any one human being could learn per lifetime. No one human being could possibly know everything! That means each of us has a very small part of all knowable knowledge. It takes a whole body of people with different bodies of knowledge coming together to protect life on earth."

About the Author

The author, Ginger Pendo, is very old at eighty years old. She's totally lost in this new tech world!

She was a nurse, an RN BSN, and that should tell about her lack in the English writing world.

In college, she was terrified of English. She didn't have a clue. Her professor, who will be acknowledged in her memoirs, made them write a lot. At the end of the quarter, she wound up with all As. "How could that be?" she asked her professor. How could I make As? I was horrible in English. In his words, he said, "Ginger, your right, your punctuation isn't really bad, your grammar is not good. Now listen to me, you have a gift of writing straight from your heart. That is a rare gift. Keep writing. Don't ever let any editor destroy your work, only help with some grammar and punctuation."

Ginger doesn't have real understanding on what he said; maybe the English world will understand what he meant.

www.ingramcontent.com/pod-product-compliance
Lightning Source LLC
LaVergne TN
LVHW091758160226
831571LV00001B/62